MONEY-SAVING ANSWERS TO YOUR CAR CARE QUESTIONS

BY BILL SIMMONS

TAB BOOKS

BLUE RIDGE SUMMIT, PA. 17214

FIRST EDITION

FIRST PRINTING—APRIL 1979

Copyright © 1979 by TAB BOOKS

Printed in the United States of America

Library of Congress Cataloging in Publication Data

Simmons, Bill.
    Money-saving answers to your car care questions.

    Includes index.
    1. Automobiles—Maintenance and repair. I. Title.
TL152.S524   629.28′8′22   78-15667
ISBN 0-8306-8978-8
ISBN 0-8306-7978-2 pbk.

Preface

In a lot of ways, owning a car in America today is like owning a two-story calliope: when it's running right, it makes beautiful music, but when it isn't, God help the poor soul who has to fix such an intricate contraption! That's pure overstatement to some people, but to many others that's the unvarnished, painful truth. Automobiles *are* getting more complex—partly because of the Clean Air Act, mostly because of the momentum of inexorable technology. And along with advancing complexity, there isn't always a corresponding increase in durability or reliability. (In the automotive industry, planned obsolescence is still a fact of life, although not yet a prime topic of conversation.) But there is something worse than technological complication—mechanics who don't understand technological complication, tinkerers rather than experts. America has plenty of competent auto mechanics, but she's also cloyed by amateurs who are just no match for today's four-wheeled fine-tuned calliopes.

Thus, more than ever before, people need answers to tough questions concerning the operation (and lack of operation!) of their own knotty, highly vulnerable automobiles. I think this book can help. It's a selective compilation of thousands of queries I have received from all over the United States, queries from people who have all kinds of car problems—common, exotic, or just plain nervewracking. I answer these questions in language that's as clear and immediate as I can make it, explaining how automotive systems works, defining terminology, pinpointing sources of trouble with as much precision as I can muster. Often a collection of symptoms suggests a range of cures, so I explore all the possibilities, remote and otherwise. If a repair is a candidate for do-it-yourselfing, I tell you how to handle it; if it's a candidate for the nearest supermechanic, I let you know—and fill you in on how much you can expect to fork over. The scope of this volume is as broad as I dare make it—covering everything from transmissions to spark plugs to pollution control devices. And I'm willing to bet that somewhere in this book, there's a piece of information that'll save you a trip to the repair shop—maybe even the poorhouse.

Bill Simmons

Contents

Chapter 1
How to Buy a Car

I want to buy a new car, probably the last I'll purchase, so I want to make a good choice. Having recently retired, I'd like a car with good gas mileage and, yet, at my age, I'd also like convenicnce and comfort. I want power steering and air conditioning. I know the latter will cut down on gas mileage, but that is only when it is in use, isn't it? I would consider a Rabbit or a Datsun but occasionally my 6-foot husband and son ride with me and they need leg room. Would you suggest some new cars that might be a good buy for someone like me?

The best compromise for your needs and wants would appear to be a car in the compact range. These include Ford Granada, Mercury Monarch, Plymouth Volare, Dodge Aspen, Chevrolet Nova, Pontiac Ventura, Olds Omega, Buick Apollo and AMC Hornet. I have tested most of these cars and find them all to be very suitable for what they are intended.

Since you desire options like air conditioning, power steering (and I assume automatic transmission and power brakes), you must choose your engine very carefully. In this range, most manufacturers offer anything from a six-cylinder in the 200-cubic-inch range up to a V-8 of about 350 cubic inches.

Many sixes will perform adequately with a few power options, but most get sluggish and actually less economical when the car is fully equipped. You might be satisfied with a large six, but my preference would be the smallest available V-8 (some GM lines offer V-6s comparable to small V-8s).

As for mileage, you should be able to get about 15 miles to the gallon in the city and possibly as high as 25 on the highway with a big six. The small V-8 will approach 15 in the city but will fall off to the low 20s on the highway.

As for air conditioning as well as the other options you want, they do affect gas mileage whether you use them or not because they add considerable weight to the vehicle. A stripped model will get 10 percent or more miles per gallon than an identical car fully equipped.

I have a 1966 Buick Electra 225 with a 445-cubic-inch engine. With 78,000 miles, it still runs good and has very quick pickup. I have a friend who wants to sell me his 1973 Buick Electra with 13,000 miles for $3,000. It doesn't have the quick acceleration that my '66 does. Is something wrong with the '73 or is this normal?

As strange as it may seem, this is normal. Starting in 1971, the government got very serious about reducing the amount of emissions from the automobile exhausts. With each year, the requirements became stricter and, until the catalytic converter arrived in 1975, the only way the manufacturers had of reducing pollutants was to make the engines run hotter and thereby burn most of them off in the combustion process. This also made the engines perform with less pep and served to reduce gasoline mileage to some degree. Since 1975, the converter serves most of this purpose by burning off the pollutants in the exhaust system. This has allowed the manufacturers to recalibrate the engines for near maximum performance and improved mileage. It also, by allowing the engines to run cooler, will make them on the average last considerably longer.

I own a 1975 Granada coupe, which was purchased because it could accommodate the height and size of my late husband (who was disabled) and the smallness of my stature. I am not getting very good mileage from the car and realize this could be due to the fact that most of my driving is short trips around the neighborhood with very little long-distance driving. I would like your advice as to the possibility of trading in the car for a smaller one that will be more economical. The Granada has 16,400 miles on it and will be 2 years old in October.

You are correct in saying that the type of driving you do is the major fact in the mileage your car delivers. I doubt very much if you would realize a significant increase in fuel mileage were you to trade for even the smallest car on the market if your driving habits remained the same. The problem is that when an engine is cold, the automatic choke adjusts to feed significantly more fuel through the carburetor than when it is at normal operating temperature. On short trips around town, the engine never gets a chance to warm up. Consequently, you are running most of the time with a very rich mixture that not only consumes more fuel, but will lead to carbon build-up in the combustion chambers and post-ignition (the engine continues to run after you've shut it off). You undoubtedly would see some improvement in mileage with a car such as a Chevette, Rabbit, or Subaru, but I don't think it would be enough to justify the money you would lose by trading a near-new car for this reason alone.

I am interested in buying a 1971 Vega. I do realize that the Vega has some problems in its initial models. I would like to know if there are any suggestions Chevrolet or yourself may have in order to keep a nice 1971 Vega in good running condition.

Despite the bad rap that Vegas have gotten in the media of late there are a lot of nice old ones out there still running quite well. And a lot of people like yourself are coming to realize that a 1971 (or 1972 or 1973) Vega in satisfactory condition is one of the best, if not the very best, transportation bargains around these days.

In a word, the cars are cheap. The negative exposure that Vegas have received has soured much of the buying public on them. General Motors, which admits to various "teething" problems with the cars, says that, in spite of it all, at least 50 percent of the early models are still functioning normally.

When you find one in good shape—as you believe you have—there is very little you have to do to keep it that way. In addition to the normal maintenance such as lubrication, oil change and tune-ups, the only thing you have to keep a close watch on is the level of the cooling fluid in the radiator.

In 1974, Chevrolet offered to install coolant catch tanks and, later, dashboard warning lights, free of charge, on all older Vegas (those items have been standard since 1974). They should be on the one you are looking at but, if not, Chevy's offer still stands.

My parents own a 1972 Vega hatchback with about 60,000 miles on it. I would like to buy it from them. The car is in very good condition aside from three small rust spots. I would like your opinion on how much it should cost and whether it's worth buying.

The retail prices of Vegas vary probably more than any other car on the market today. This is because of the reputation the car earned in its early years.

If the car is as sound as you say it is and, considering you know the kind of care it has gotten over the years, I would say that $700 would be a fair price for all concerned.

Could you give me some advice on an Aspen station wagon? I want to get one with air conditioning and would like to know whether I need an eight-cylinder engine or can I get away with the six. What are the gas mileage differences between the two engines?

A couple of years ago, I would have advised the 318 V-8 because the single-barrel 225 six just doesn't have enough power to give reasonable performance when the car has options such as air conditioning, automatic transmission, etc.

In 1977, however, Dodge introduced a two-barrel version of the 225 that provides an acceptable compromise and should be sufficient unless you're looking for real acceleration. It's standard on the wagons. Fuel mileage difference, according to the EPA, is about one mile per gallon.

I own a 1972 Vega that has been driven 42,000 miles and is developing some body rust. Is it economical to have the rust removed and the car painted or should I purchase a new automobile? I am asking because I have heard that due to the aluminum engine, Vegas develop problems after 50,000 miles. Otherwise, the car is in good mechanical condition.

I think the answer to your question centers on your financial situation. As your car now stands, it probably is worth somewhere between $300 and $500 which, on a trade-in, would just about cover the additional costs such as taxes, title, and tags.

If you can afford it and have a yen for a new car, by all means go ahead. But, with apologies to the legions of Vega haters, should money be a serious consideration, I would have no qualms about spending a couple of hundred to dress up the Vega and go on using it.

As has been said so many times before, there were many cases of serious engine problems in early Vegas, including 1972 models. However, those troubles invariably showed up long before 42,000 miles. And, despite its reputation, the aluminum Vega when right has a lower incidence of repair than any other General Motors engine. I believe that if you have gotten 42,000 relatively trouble-free miles from your Vega, the chances are good that there are many more miles left in the car.

It would seem that you are confusing the mileage with the five-year, 50,000-mile warranty that was offered on Vega engines. There's no correlation.

As to the body work, should you decide to go that way, make sure that the person who does the job gets all the rust, even if it means more extensive repairs. If any is left, it'll come back to haunt you faster than you can imagine.

I recently ordered a 1977 Dodge Aspen SE (Special Edition) with six-cylinder engine. Now I have been told that I would have saved money by ordering a Plymouth Volare Premier. Is there any difference in the cars or just the price, and would I have saved gas by ordering the two-barrel carburetor instead of the single?

The price you pay for the car really comes down to the dealer. Throughout the various lines of Aspen and Volare, the Aspen has a base list price of $12 more than Volare. And the list prices for options also are the same.

As to differences in the cars, they are so minimal as to be nonexistent. Aspens and Volares come down the same assembly line one after another. The main differences are in the trim—shapes of the grilles for example.

As to the two-barrel carburetor versus single, the latter should prove quite satisfactory on models that are not heavily loaded with options. If, however, the car has automatic transmission, power steering, power brakes, and air conditioning, the two-barrel could prove as economical or more so because it is more efficient. It certainly would have better performance.

Since I am not mechanically inclined, I wonder if you could give me some information on how to buy a good used car and on what kind of books I could get to learn to repair my own car.

The best advice I can give anyone in the area of used cars is to pay a qualified mechanic, if necessary, to check it out. Any reputable dealer with nothing to hide will permit this. As to repairs, you must learn to walk before you can run. A good start is *Basic Auto Maintenance,* published by Chilton of Radnor, Pa. TAB Books of Blue Ridge Summit, Pa. also publishes auto repair manuals: Check out their latest—book nos. 978 and 949.

Chapter 2
Engines: Searching
for Better Performance

We have a family of four boys and need our Olds station wagon which gets about 14 miles per gallon on trips. I had a 1952 Olds 88 that got better than 17 mpg. Although that was some years ago, it concerns me that the auto companies are supposed to have made improvements but the cars use more gas.

I have heard that carburetors have been developed to give better gas mileage but that the oil companies keep them off the market to keep gasoline sales high. Is there any truth to this?

Rumors like that have been flying for decades and also include stories of a magic pill that can turn water into gasoline in your tank. Granted, there have been improvements in carburetor design over the years, but there have been no revolutionary breakthroughs as you seem to indicate.

Additionally, there are a lot of fly-by-night companies offering all kinds of valves, sparkplugs and other gimmics alleged to give you "10 to 30 percent" better gas mileage. Don't believe it.

Changes are coming, however. I recently witnessed a fuel management system that converts any engine to stratified charge with resultant increase in fuel economy, decrease in emissions, and improvement in performance. Whether it will work in mass production, only time will tell.

I am planning to take a long trip in a VW Camper and would like to know if it is possible or practical to convert the engine to use propane instead of gasoline. I am told there is a conversion kit available. Any suggestions?

I understand that several tests have been undertaken and it is feasible to use propane as a substitute for gasoline in internal combustion engines. But it is not really a practical application. Conversion is relatively expensive, fuel mileage does not come up to that obtained by the same engine on gasoline, and fuel availability is not good (although most campgrounds do have supplies). I wouldn't recommend it.

Is it safe to add gasoline additives to unleaded gas for use in my 1977 Oldsmobile 98 Regency. I've heard yes and no and want to be safe.

The only way to be sure is to check the ingredients on the label. If lead is included, don't use it as it can damage the catalytic converter. If ingredients aren't listed, don't take a chance.

I am planning on replacing the 350-cubic-inch engine in my 1971 Chevrolet Impala. I would like to know if I can use a 1972 or 1973 engine or even go to a smaller engine to improve the gasoline mileage. I drive about 6,000 miles per month in my business.

Driving that much—72,000 miles a year if my multiplication is correct—the existing engine must be the most durable in history. Or maybe you just got the car. Either way, you can use just about any Chevrolet 350 up to and including 1976 models. However, due to methods of controlling pollution, a 1972 or 1973 will give you worse mileage than a 1971. Also, a 305 will bolt up without major modifications and, since most of your driving must be on open highways, should significantly increase your gas mileage.

I would like to know if a certain product sold by a mail order house is worth purchasing. They are called fire injectors, and the literature says they are the greatest invention in the auto industry in 50 years. They supposedly give a greater explosion, causing more power, leaving less unburned gas to wear down pistons as a result of diluted lubricant. What do you say?

I would say that the person who wrote the literature was, at least, given to exaggeration. It's safe to say we have had a few automotive inventions of more importance in the last 50 years, like hydraulic brakes (and later power disc brakes), fuel injection, automatic transmission, collapsible steering columns, seat belts, and so on.

Back to your fire injectors. They do work. I can say that from experience. They do not, however, seem to work any better than standard spark plugs. They also do not seem to last any longer.

As to leaving less unburned gas in the cylinders, I doubt that statement very much. The only time you have any unburned fuel-air mixture is when a plug isn't firing at all. Granted, there is a great amount of unburned hydrocarbons, which are the major cause of automotive pollutants, but they can hardly be considered as fuel.

There is a way to greatly reduce the amount of unburned hydrocarbons in an engine, but it has nothing to do with trick plugs. Honda has just such an engine—what it calls the CVCC. The secret is revising the shape of the combustion chamber and setting off the explosion in a small firing chamber, allowing it to swirl through the rest of the cylinder.

The best I can say about your fire injectors is that they won't hurt anything.

I have read that Chrysler has a new motor called Lean Burn that doesn't require any catalytic converter or hoses and runs on regular gas. Could you tell me where I can get information?

Chrysler's lean-burn engine refers to a series of engine modifications and precise electronic controls of the firing of the charge in the combustion chamber. This permits the engine to run on a lean air-to-fuel ratio of about

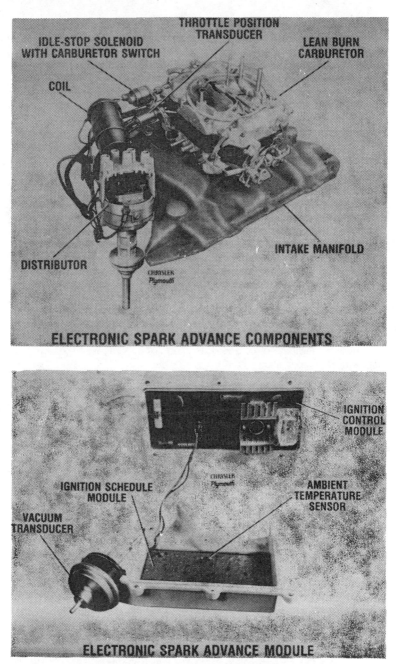

ELECTRONIC SPARK ADVANCE COMPONENTS

THROTTLE POSITION TRANSDUCER

IDLE-STOP SOLENOID WITH CARBURETOR SWITCH

LEAN BURN CARBURETOR

COIL

INTAKE MANIFOLD

DISTRIBUTOR

CHRYSLER Plymouth

ELECTRONIC SPARK ADVANCE MODULE

IGNITION CONTROL MODULE

IGNITION SCHEDULE MODULE

CHRYSLER Plymouth

AMBIENT TEMPERATURE SENSOR

VACUUM TRANSDUCER

Fig. 2-1. Through the use of various sensors and transistorized assemblies, the lean-burn system fires plugs at the optimum moment, reducing emissions and slightly increasing fuel economy. (Courtesy Chrysler Corp.)

18:1 (as compared to the average engine's 14:1) for better fuel economy and emissions control.

The heart of the lean-burn system is electronic spark (Fig. 2-1) recently developed by Chrysler engineers. Sensors in the engine monitor the factors that affect emissions, fuel economy, and engine performance in the areas of temperatures and engine speeds.

That information is fed to an onboard computer that calculates the precise moment when the charge should be fired for the best balance of power, emissions and fuel economy.

I am interested in Chrysler Corporation's lean-burn engine. Has this new system lived up to Chrysler's expectations and what, if any, problems have arisen? More importantly, does Chrysler have any plans to extend this system to the 360 and 318 V-8 engines and, if so, when will they be available in the Volare and Aspen models?

So far, the engine has proven to be very reliable. It was introduced in the 1976 model year only on the 400-cubic-inch V-8 and was available only in intermediates and full-size cars.

For 1977, Chrysler has adapted the lean-burn to its 400 and 360 four-barrel engines and hopes to receive EPA certification for the two-barrel 318.

As for availability, the 360 two-barrel now is offered in only coupe versions of the Aspen and Volare. It also can be had in the police version of the four-door sedan.

After certification, of course, the lean-burn 318 will be offered in all models of the Aspen and Volare.

I would like to know what is the difference between large and small 6-cylinder engines and which cars offer the large 6. I also understand that some General Motors lines offer V-6 engines that are comparable to small V-8s. Would you please explain?

Basically, the differences between large and small engines—be they 4s, 6s, or 8s—is the amount of fuel they consume and the amount of power they produce. All, obviously, are compromises of one sort or another. The reason for this is that fuel economy and power are mutually exclusive. Six-cylinder engines (Fig. 2-2) are most prevalent in compact cars although they are available in some intermediates. All builders of American compacts offer various engine options—some more than others. For example, Ford (and Mercury) offer the choice of a 140-cubic-inch 4 or a 200-cubic-inch 6 or a 302 cubic inch V8 in the Fairmont/Zephyr lines. Chrysler, however has two versions of its 225-cubic-inch 6 for its Volare/Aspen compacts. Most GM divisions offer two engine choices in their compacts also. The smaller engines are intended for cars that are not loaded with accessories where they perform adequately under most circumstances. Since extras like air conditioning, automatic transmission, power steering, power brakes, and so forth depend on a percentage of engine output, the small engines can actually be less efficient than a larger one in such an application. The bigger 6 works well when a few options are included. But, for a fully loaded car, it is advisable to get at least a small V-8, most of which are in the 300-cid range. GM's 231-cubic-in V-6 is offered in some Pontiac, Oldsmobile, and Buick models and is comparable to Oldsmobile's 260 cubic-inch V-8.

Fig. 2-2. In-line six-cylinder engines have been an industry staple for years. But shorter V-6s are replacing them because they take up less space, allowing shorter (and lighter) engine compartments. (Courtesy AMC)

I recently read about small Japanese diesel engines that are being installed in small pickup trucks. Are there any diesel engines available that can be adapted to an American pickup?

International-Harvester has a line of diesel-powered vehicles in the size range you are interested in. The engines are built by Nissan of Japan (Datsun in the United States). You might check an I-H dealer to see if the engines are available by themselves. Last year Oldsmobile division of General Motors introduced a 350-cubic inch V8 diesel for Chevrolet and GMC pickup trucks. Volkswagen also has introduced a diesel version of its popular Rabbit (Fig. 2-3).

Diesel engines are considerably more expensive than comparable gasoline engines. The Chevrolet and GMC pickups, for instance, are about $800 more with the diesel engine. This is offset, however, by reduced operating costs in both fuel and service.

I own a 1974 Mazda RX-4 with 19,000 miles and a 1972 RX-2 with 38,000 miles. The Mazda rotary engine is one of the most fantastic I've ever seen in terms of reliability and power. Gas consumption is not out of line with regard to horsepower output.

I have read with curiosity that Detroit has dropped the whole rotary concept cold. What's their problem? Based on my limited experience with the rotary, I see no insurmountable problem. Even the rotary's somewhat thirsty nature has been cutback. I can't help but believe that Detroit's throwing of cold water on the rotary will cause a general panic in the advisability of investing in such a car. Do you have any comments?

Although Mazda has made some marked improvements in the fuel mileage of its rotary engines, it still doesn't compare favorably with the mileage being obtained by less powerful but otherwise comparable piston engined cars. As government requirements for mileage increase, this will become a bigger factor.

Even more important, however, is the fact that by its very nature, the rotary is a dirty engine. For its size and power output, the rotary delivers considerably more pollutants to the exhaust system.

Mazda has tried to tackle this problem by using a thermo-reactor that works like an afterburner. By funneling the exhaust gasses through a very high temperature area, most of the pollutants are burned off. But the government is requiring less and less pollutants over the long haul, and cleaning the rotary's exhaust will create a large problem as time goes on.

Take those already formidable handicaps and add the phenomenal cost of development, design, and tooling and there is an investment that General Motors did not feel it was up to making.

Incidentally, Mercedes must be thinking along the same lines. It developed the C-111 with a multiple rotary a couple of years ago and, the last anybody saw of the car, it was setting several land-speed records with a diesel engine.

We have a controversy at work as to the proper length of time to warm up a car. I am on the side of minimum warmup—approximately 5 seconds in warm weather, 10 seconds in colder weather—then operation below 55 miles per hour for up to 10 minutes. This keeps condensation to a minimum.

The other side believes a car should warm up approximately 2 to 10 minutes depending on temperature. They then operate below 55 mph for at least another 5 minutes. They claim this cuts wear and avoids high stresses in their engine and shafts.

Please settle this argument for peace of mind and as a benefit to everyone's cars.

You've got the situation surrounded. You are on the short side and your compatriots are on the long side. We'll take your too-brief warmup period first. When you don't give a car enough time to get warm, excessive wear develops. Five to 10 seconds is not enough to circulate the oil through the engine or to get the fluid moving in the transmission. This can cut up to 10 percent from a car's anticipated lifespan.

Your cohorts, meanwhile, are wasting fuel and, as you contend, allowing condensation to build up in the engine oil sump. The wasted fuel speaks for itself—mainly in money. But the condensation can, at best, necessitate more frequent oil changes and, at worst, lead to internal engine problems over the years.

Although some cars have their individual idiosyncrasies, the general rule of thumb is to allow the engine to fast idle (with your foot off the

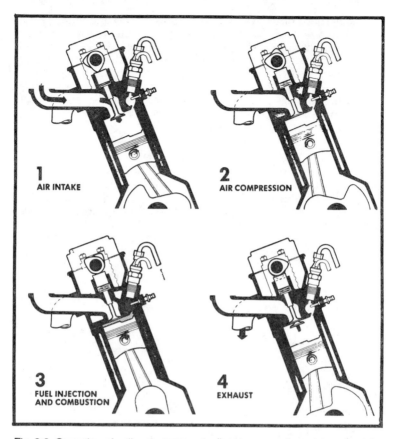

Fig. 2-3. Operation of a diesel engine actually is less complicated than that of a comparable gasoline engine. The main difference is the absence of an ignition system. (Courtesy Volkswagen).

accelerator) for about a minute when the outside temperature is above freezing. As it gets colder, it is best to let things warm up for about two minutes. This is necessitated more by the requirements of the transmission fluid. When it is bitterly cold and you get the engine started and immediately put the transmission in gear, many times the car won't move. A two-minute period will get the fluid circulating and build the needed pressure to make the transmission work.

After the prescribed warmup period, it is advisable to keep engine revolutions under 4,000 per minute until the coolant reaches normal operating temperature. For those unfortunate enough to have a car without a temperature gauge, this usually takes from 5 to 15 minutes, depending on atmospheric conditions.

A friend and I disagree on the status of his 1971 Trans Am with a 455 HO engine. He claims that through the removal of air conditioning and by replacing standard dual exhausts with 2 1/2-inch side pipes, he has added 130 horsepower to 390.

I say that Pontiac rates that engine at 360 and what he did might increase horsepower, but not by that much. Who is right? You're both wrong. But you are closer to being right. Pontiac offered two 455s back then—one rated at 365 horsepower (10-to-1 compression) and the other at 390 (10.25-to-1). Removing the air conditioning would have little effect on engine horsepower, although shedding the weight might increase usable power. Installation of a free-flow exhaust, including tubular headers, could add 10 percent. But nothing like 130 horsepower.

I recently bought a 1977 Oldsmobile Delta 88 Royale and find I have a Chevrolet engine in the car. I have no complaints with the car but would like to know the differences in the two engines. There are many differences, most of them what I would call subtle. For instance, the Chevrolet LM-1 engine that is being installed in most Delta 88 models reaches a maximum torque output of 270 foot/pounds at 2,400 revolutions per minute. The Olds L34 reaches 275 foot/pounds at 2,000 rpm. Maximum horsepower for both engines is 170 at 3,800 rpm.

The L34, which is offered in all other Olds models with the exception of the subcompact Starfire coupe and in Deltas sold in California or high-altitude, has a compression ratio of 8.0-to-1 while the LM-1 is 8.5-to-1.

Although both engines have a displacement of 350 cubic inches and are fed through four-barrel carburetors, there is a slight difference in the bore and stroke. The Olds bore is 4.057 inches and the stroke is 3.385 inches. On the Chevy, it's 4.0 and 3.48.

There also is a difference in the mileage rating of the two engines by the Environmental Protection Agency. The Olds L34 is rated at 16 city and 22 highway with a combined 18. The LM-1 comes in at 15 city, 20 highway and 17 combined.

Although most of the queries I received on this subject concerned the above, one reader claimed that, in addition to the Chevrolet engine, his Delta 88 also came equipped with a different transmission than that found in other cars. He said he had a transmission designated as THM-200, rather than the standard Olds THM-350. He is correct in that he has a THM-200. However, that is the only transmission available in any Delta 88, regardless of engine with the exception of the Custom Cruiser wagons where the THM-350 is standard. The THM-350 also is standard on all 98s.

And, as if the situation isn't muddled enough, GM is being attacked for using some Chevrolet engines in both Pontiacs and Buicks. Although nobody has complained yet, there are many other instances of engine sharing—Olds engines in Pontiacs, Buicks, and Cadillacs (Seville only and with modifications), Buick engines in Pontiacs and Oldsmobiles, and Pontiac engines in Buicks. In fact, the only division that produced all of its own engines is Chevrolet.

Actually, it's a wonder nobody is complaining about the rest of the cars. All of GM's B-body cars—Chevrolet Impala and Caprice, Pontiac Catalina and Bonneville, Buick LeSabre and Olds Delta 88—are built of many of the same pieces on the same assembly lines. The same thing is true throughout all of the various car classifications.

And then there are Ford and Chrysler which several years ago established engine and drive train divisions separate from the car divisions and now install the same engines through their various lines.

Legally, the complaint isn't so much with what GM did, but how it went about it. As New York Attorney General Louis Lefkowitz pointed out in bringing suit against GM, the company's failure to disclose the practice in advertising constitutes false advertising, and, therefore, deceptive business practices.

Oldsmobile continues to offer only the LM-1 in 49-state versions of the Delta 88. But signs are all over every dealership to make sure the customer knows in advance what he's getting.

Beginning with the 1978 model year, Oldsmobile has installed only the L34 in its 88's, while the new scaled-down Cutlass uses a Chevrolet built 305-cubic inch V8.

I have a 1976 Chrysler Cordoba with the 400-cubic-inch lean-burn engine. Basically I am very happy with the combination. The car has good response, acceptable fuel economy, and fine performance.

Recently, however, I was returning home in the evening and the car began to run roughly. I stopped at a service station near my home and asked for help. The mechanic opened the hood, took one look, and told me he had no idea how to fix my electronically-monitored engine. Fortunately, it ran well enough to get me home and to my dealer the next day where they were able to straighten it out in minutes by replacing the "little black box."

The possibilities have me worried though. Suppose it should stop completely somewhere on a Saturday when the dealers are closed. Is there any way a garage mechanic can check things out to get the car running again, or would I be stuck until a Monday morning?

There is a procedure that is spelled out quite clearly in the Chrysler service manual for checking out the system. It also is detailed in such publications as Chilton's *Auto Repair Manual,* which many garages keep on hand for reference.

There is, however, a fly in the ointment. At the end of the test procedures for both a non-running engine and a poorly running engine, the mechanic is told to replace the spark control computer if all else has failed.

Since this device is still in its infancy, it is highly unlikely that your average repair shop will have them on hand as yet. If you do a lot of driving in inopportune times in inopportune places, it might give you peace of mind to carry a spare yourself.

I have a 1969 Buick LeSabre and a 1972 Chrysler Newport, both with high-compression engines requiring premium gasoline. Since premium is getting harder to find and more expensive, I was wondering if either or both of these cars can be converted to operate efficiently on unleaded or regular fuel.

The answer is yes; both can be converted to run on regular, but the cost would be outrageous. Among the things you would probably have to change are cylinder heads and pistons (to lower the compression ratio), the camshaft, and the exhaust valve seats. You'd have to detune the engine too.

A project like that, depending on who does it and whether they use new, reconditioned, or used parts, would cost anywhere from $600 to $1,000. If the cars mean so much to you that you are willing to spend that kind of money, you'd be better off having rebuilt late model low-compression versions of the same engines put in. You could even look into buying and installing late-model used engines.

In our office there are four different General Motors cars—Chevelle, Le Sabre, Seville, and Monte Carlo. Since all have a 350-cubic-inch engine, I would like to know if it is the same engine in all four cars.

Each division of General Motors has its own version of the 350-cubic-inch engine, and each version varies in rather subtle ways. Therefore, since the Chevelle and Monte Carlo are both Chevrolet products, they are equipped with the same basic engine, while the Buick and Cadillac versions differ. There are considerable variations in the fuel, ignition, and cooling systems. As an example, the Seville engine is the only GM-350 to use fuel injection instead of carburetors. Incidentally, Cadillac buys the basic 350 blocks from Oldsmobile Division and dresses them to its own specifications.

My son is planning on dropping a Chrysler Hemi 396 engine into a 1971 Plymouth Duster. He says he can do this without any problem. Do you have any comments as to whether there could be some problems in putting this heavier engine into the Duster.

There is a lot more to it than "dropping" it in, and there are problems to be faced later on. For starters, he'll need a bigger radiator (increased cooling capacity), a heavy-duty transmission (to handle the increased torque), different engine mounts, linkage, wiring, and exhaust system. Most of all is the safety aspect. To make it handle and stop properly, it'll need bigger wheels, tires, and brakes, heavier suspension pieces, better shocks, and an increased torsion-bar rate.

Can you tell me specifically what it is that people don't do for their Vega engines that they should? Is the lack of water the only thing that damages the engine? And what are the advantages of this aluminum alloy engine over a cast iron one?

Lack of the proper amount of coolant is the primary reason for most troubles with the aluminum 140-cubic-inch, four-cylinder engine now used in several small Chevrolet and Pontiac models.

Under excessive temperatures, both aluminum and cast iron tend to expand and, in many cases, warp. The difference is the cast iron almost always regains its original configuration upon cooling, while aluminum stays distorted. This causes the main problem—blowing of head gaskets—which can only be corrected by resurfacing the warped part, block and cylinder head.

General Motors engineers have installed both catch tanks and interior warning devices that inform the driver of excessive coolant loss. The company obviously feels it has overcome the problem since it is offering a five-year, 60,000-mile warranty on the engine.

Like any other engine, the aluminum four requires other basic maintenance such as tune-ups and oil changes to perform properly.

The advantage you ask about is primarily in weight. It permits further savings through the use of lighter suspension and frame components—all in the interest of fuel economy.

I have two questions concerning modifications to my 1972 Pinto Runabout. First, I'd like to know if I can "bolt in" a 2,300-cc engine in place of the original 2,000. Secondly, is there any way I can achieve a quicker steering ratio? The car has numerous suspension modifications which enable it to react more precisely to

steering inputs, but the slow steering ratio is now the limiting factor.

The swap is considerably more than a bolt-in operation because the bell-housing bolt patterns differ. This would require, at the very least, an engine-transmission adapter. It's doubtful if the performance results would make it worthwhile. You would be better off installing performance options—starting with a free-flow exhaust system—on the 2,000. As for the steering ratio, Ford has no optional parts, but different gears might be available from your local supplier of competition parts.

What do you think the chances are of shoehorning a V-8 engine into an older Ford Pinto? I have the pieces and would like to give it a try.

You may think you have the pieces but you don't. The biggest problem with your idea is the fact that the front suspension will not support the added weight of the V-8 engine. If you are determined to do the conversion, you should adapt the entire front suspension from an older Mustang. Also, you'll have to buy or make engine-mount adapters, engine-to-transmission adapters, and a different length drive shaft. A heavier duty radiator is in order too.

Chapter 3
Engines: Troubles on the Inside

I have a 1973 Mercury Montego V-8. The service manager says it may need a timing chain. Compression is 60-65-65-60-70-50-60-70. How can I tell without doing an expensive overhaul?

Timing chain slack (stretching) shows up as an inability to maintain timing. However, it has nothing to do with compression which, in your case, reveals a serious problem on cylinder six. A disparity of more than 10 pounds over all cylinders indicates either valve or ring failure.

In October, while traveling in Virginia, the crankshaft failed on our 1974 Buick LeSabre (46,000 miles). Thus far, no action by us will convince General Motors to reimburse the $1,160 repair bill.

We tried to recover the defective part, but the mechanic in Virginia had discarded it after my dealer had requested it be returned for inspection.

We have contacted the zone managers, written to Buick headquarters in Flint, Mich., and were referred to the local zones. What now?

Chalk it up to experience, albiet expensive and unpleasant. Without the defective part, you don't have (excuse the pun) a crankshaft to stand on. Even if you had it, I doubt if Buick would assume liability on a car that's more than a year and some 34,000 miles out of warranty.

Last summer I drove my 1975 Ford Granada at high speed on the highway for about 100 miles with the air conditioner on and the automatic transmission in "2" rather than in "Drive." Now, with the car having about 28,000 miles on it, I notice that it's using oil. I'm getting about 1,000 to 1,500 miles per quart of oil. Do you think there is any connection?

There are some variables here. The biggest question is what you mean by high speed. If you mean the legal speed limit of 55 miles per hour, I doubt if you would have done the engine any serious damage, assuming everything else was in proper order at the time. Running at 65 − 70 mph or higher in second gear for that distance could put an undue strain on the engine and result in the wearing of parts to cause oil burning.

The old rule of thumb used to be that it was normal for an engine to burn a quart of oil between oil changes. But manufacturers today are recommending changes at 5,000-mile (or more) intervals, and I think most people will find themselves adding a quart or two between changes as mileage builds up.

By this I mean that the engine's oil consumption rate is within acceptable bounds. But should it get worse you might wish to have a compression check done (dry followed by wet) to determine where the problem lies.

My 4-year-old imported compact is losing oil. I see spots of oil on the pavement where I park it and lately have had to add as much as 2 quarts every week. A mechanic told me it's a bad rear seal and would be expensive to repair. Any suggestions?

If it is the engine's rear main seal, it can be quite expensive to repair since it usually involves removal of the transmission and disassembly of the bottom end of the engine. This entails dropping the oil pan (which sometimes can include disconnecting front suspension pieces) and removing all rod and main bearing caps. The crankshaft is then lowered and the new seal, (which might cost as much as 75 cents) is inserted. Done in this manner, the job can cost as much as $200 to $300.

There is a cheaper way that often works, but it cannot be applied to all types of cars. This includes dropping the oil pan and removing the rear main bearing cap. The new seal is then worked into the journal up and around the top of the crank throw and with the old seal being forced out in the process. If this can be done to your engine, it should cost less than $100.

It's obvious from your letter that you are hoping that there is some kind of sealant—such as those that have been used to close radiator leaks—that would solve your problem. Unfortunately there is no miracle additive.

Your other alternatives are to sell or trade in the car or to continue to use it and shop around to make bulk purchases of the cheapest available oil.

My 1972 Ford pickup truck (360 engine) has been behaving strangely for some time: after coasting from about 40 mph to about 25 mph, the engine goes dead when I apply light throttle to accelerate. It also backfires through the carburetor.

Only by applying full throttle or by downshifting will it catch hold and resume acceleration. I have replaced the ignition system wires, plugs, points, and distributor cap: no improvement. I have also checked the timing, and the vacuum advance is functioning okay. I have replaced the carburetor air filter and checked the PCV valve.

The truck runs reasonably well at highway speeds, getting 10 miles per gallon pulling a trailer. Do you have any ideas?

Assuming you have *properly* done all the work you say and the truck still performs only reasonably well at steady highway speeds, I would look a little deeper.

When you say it backfires through the carburetor, I am inclined to think you might have a damaged intake valve on one or more cylinders. This would cause all the symptoms you describe.

I would recommend a compression check, which is a simple operation. After removing the plugs (and getting the ignition wires out of the way to avoid a shock), insert the compression gauge tightly in each plug hole and crank the engine. Don't worry too much about the numbers you get. Each cylinder should read within 10 pounds of the others. Should a discrepancy arise, do it again, adding a little oil to each cylinder (to check rings). If it's still bad, valves are your problem.

The engine in my 1969 Thunderbird seems to have lost power, and it makes a sporadic hissing noise. It doesn't seem to be misfiring or running roughly, just with less response. Can you tell me what the problem is?

I hate to be the bearer of bad tidings, but your description leads me to believe you have blown a head gasket (or two). The head gasket (Fig. 3-1) is a thin piece of metal—usually a copper or aluminum alloy—that is used to seal the juncture of the cylinder head with the engine block. Its main purpose is to insure compression of the fuel-air mixture in the cylinders, but it also keeps the lubricants and coolants in the proper channels.

It sounds as though you have blown a gasket from the compression area to the outside, since you hear a sporadic hissing noise. This means that each time the piston comes up on the compression stroke, it is pushing the fuel-air mixture through the gasket leak and out of the engine.

This is perhaps the easiest headgasket malfunction to discover. Other points of failure include cylinder to an oil or coolant journal or both.

It is a fairly expensive job to replace a head gasket, requiring the removal of certain accessories, the valve-cover gasket, the rocker-arm assembly and pushrods, along with the cylinder head itself.

To be certain this is the trouble and, if so, to determine in which bank the failure has occurred, a compression check should be done. This is a fairly simple test in which a compression gauge ($5 or less) is inserted in the spark plug holes, one at a time, and the engine cranked over. The readings should be in the same range if everything is normal. If one cylinder registers more than 20 pounds less than the average, it is the one with the leak.

I own a 1974 Volkswagen and there are knocks in the engine. I have listened to other VW engines and do not hear these knocks. In fact, the average VW engine sounds pretty quiet to me. I have taken my car to two Volkswagen dealers, and they also hear the knocks but tell me not to worry about them. I do worry about them—my engine warranty runs out next year. Do you have any idea what causes the knocks and what can be done about it?

There are a couple of conditions at the back of the venerable Beetle that, in many instances, cause rattles that sound like knocks. First is the position of the air cleaner. If it isn't perfect, it will bang against the deck lid, making a knocking sound. To check this, lift the deck lid and listen. If the noise is gone, that's it. Another possibility is the muffler. Sometimes the placement of the muffler is such that the right-hand corner can bang against the surrounding metal, causing a knocking noise.

If it isn't either of these, a VW instructor advises, you probably have internal problems. There have been cases where a VW engine has been diagnosed as having a rod knock and it turns out only to be a loose rocker arm inside the valve cover. Whatever, I would check out the possibilities as soon as possible to insure against any serious problems.

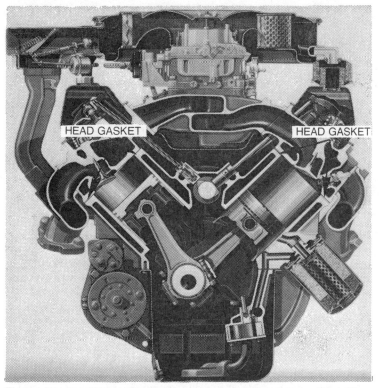

Fig. 3-1. Head gaskets are fitted between cylinder heads and engine block. They don't fail often. But when they do, it's major. (Courtesy Ford)

I own a 1972 Toyota Corona with automatic transmission and air conditioning. After 27,000 miles, I need a valve job. Can you give me any idea what the parts and labor would cost me?

The cost should be between $125 and $250, depending on who does the work and what needs to be done. If all eight valves (one intake and one exhaust for each of the four cylinders) must be replaced, the cost will be greater. Usually, the valves can be ground and reseated.

A valve job is the simplest internal engine repair to do for the mechanic who has the proper equipment. All external accessories must be removed along with the valve cover and rocker arm assembly. Then the head is removed, dismantled, and serviced before the procedure is reversed.

My mechanic tells me that compression in the cylinders of my car is lower than it should be. He said I probably need new cylinder rings. The car has 52,000 miles on it. Isn't this rather soon for a ring job and couldn't there be another reason for the low compression?

There are two things that can cause compression loss. One is failure of the piston rings; the other is the need for a valve job. To check on what the cause is, squirt some motor oil in each cylinder and test the compression

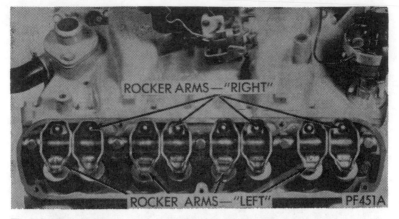

Fig. 3-2. "Tapping" in an engine can often be cured by adjusting the rocker arms under the valve covers. (Courtesy Chrysler Corp.)

again. If it rises, the trouble is in the rings; if not, it's valves. As for the mileage, that is not particularly out of line for such a problem. It all depends on how the car has been used and maintained.

I have a 1971 Chevrolet Impala with 24,000 miles on it. Very often while idling, the engine is very noisy. It sounds like the tapping of a number of typewriters. Could you tell me what is causing this so I can have it corrected?

This tapping you hear is caused by what mechanics refer to as "slop in the valve train." I would presume that the engine in your car is a six-cylinder because they are most prone to valve tapping. It does, however, occur occasionally in Chevy V-8s as well as other makes.

The chances are that you can eliminate the noise by having a mechanic adjust the valves, which is a fairly simple procedure. Sometimes, particularly when a car is driven most of the time on short trips at lower speeds or when the oil isn't changed at regular intervals, sludge can build up in the hydraulic lifters, which makes proper adjustment at the rocker-arm assembly (Fig. 3-2). Next to impossible, replacing the lifters is much more of a job than adjustment. Either way, you should have it attended to before more serious valve damage results.

I have a fantastic 1972 GL Subaru. Lately I have noticed a puff of blue smoke when I first start out. This clears up in about a block of driving. It reoccurs occasionally when I start up after a traffic light. Everything runs smooth and I get good gas and oil mileage. I have about 54,000 trouble-free miles on my car. Can you help?

Your problem, if it can be called that at this stage, is normal wear and tear. What probably is happening is that the piston rings in your car are starting to wear, allowing slight amounts of engine oil to seep into the combustion chamber, causing the blue smoke. This problem always is most noticeable on acceleration from a standing start and, as it progresses, on deceleration in gear. I would suggest that you continue to operate and maintain the car as you have in the past, paying regular attention to the level of oil in the crankcase. It will gradually begin to use more oil. That is, unless you are a perfectionist with money to burn, in which case you can drop a couple hundred dollars on a ring job.

I have a 1968 Ford (302 V-8) that served me quite well for several years. Recently, after being run earlier in the day, the car just flatly refused to start. I tried everything I could think of—checking that there was spark, making sure that there was fuel flow through the carburetor, even giving it a shot of ether. When it still wouldn't start, I had it towed to a service station. The mechanic got it running, but it is really down on power and, on occasions, still refuses to start. He said the engine is about worn out and that I shouldn't use the car for anything more than trips to the store. I later tried to set the timing to make it run better and couldn't get the matchup points to stay in one spot. Can you explain why it would go from operating just fine to apparently junk just like that?

The whole answer may be in your statement about not being able to time the car because the marks keep jumping around. This indicates slop or slack in the timing chain (Fig. 3-3). Over the years and miles, any chain has a tendency to stretch. Eventually it gets to the point where this stretching renders it useless—like a bicycle chain that slips off the sprockets.

In this case, the timing chain, which is supposed to match up the turning of the camshaft with that of the crankshaft, isn't doing the job. Therefore, the intake and exhaust valves aren't opening and closing precisely at the required moment and the distributor, which is driven off the camshaft, isn't delivering spark at the proper instant.

There is one positive factor. Since the car still runs, the chain hasn't broken. If it had, you would have done considerable damage to the valve train and rendered it virtually worthless. The way it is now, you could get it running properly again by having the chain replaced at a cost of about $200. But make sure the condition of the car warrants such an investment.

Fig. 3-3. Proper tension in the timing chain is very important. If excessive play develops with age, it will be impossible to maintain proper ignition timing. (Courtesy Chrysler Corp.)

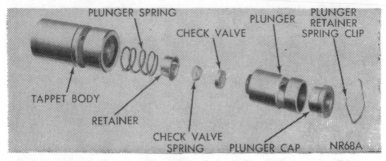

Fig. 3-4. Hydraulic lifters (two for every cylinder in the engine) are small items. But if they become fouled, tapping noises will result. (Courtesy Chrysler Corp.)

I have a 1966 Mustang with a 289 V-8 engine. For about four months I have noticed a loud-ticking sound when the car is warmed up and idling, much like the sound of a typewriter.

Since most people told me it was due to valve trouble, I proceeded to adjust the valves to specifications, but the sound remains. I also cannot properly set the idle, since the engine begins to shake violently below 850 revolutions per minute. Are the two problems related and will I have to put in an entire set of lifters? I have 97,000 miles on the car.

With 97,000 miles on the car and persistent valve tap, I would say your problem more than likely is the hydraulic lifters (Fig. 3-4).. They are probably gummed up to the point that they are working like solid lifters, making accurate adjustment impossible. I certainly would replace the lifters, and if you're so inclined, give the heads to a reputable machine shop for a routine valve job.

My 1974 Chevrolet recently had to have a completely new motor because one of the wristpins protruded from the piston and gouged a channel in the block. It cost almost $1,000 at the local dealer's shop.

The service manager assured me that it was a factory defect and that he thought Chevrolet would repay me. But the factory representative refused to pay, giving only the curt response, "It's out of warranty." Is there somewhere we can turn?

It would seem that since what happened is so unusual, the piece (Fig. 3-5) probably was defective to start with. However, that is the purpose of a warranty, and when something like this happens after the warranty expires, the manufacturer can't legally be held responsible.

You do have a right to complain to the dealer, however. No competent service manager can honestly say a company will pay for damage to a car he knows is out of warranty. And $1,000 is an outrageous price since a rebuilt shortblock could have been installed for little more than half that.

I have a 1965 Rambler Classic with a six-cylinder engine. I have this bad tapping in the engine, which the Rambler mechanic said was caused by bad valves.

He put in all new valves and changed the oil and filter, but it still taps, worse than before. I thought if the valves were changed, it would correct the noise. Is there anything that can be done?

28

I am not saying that the valves in your car's engine didn't need to be changed, but the chances are very slim that they caused or are causing the tapping noise you hear. In cases like this, the tapping is caused by improper adjustment of the clearance between the pushrods and the rocker arms (which then activate the valves).

The cause almost invariably can be linked to not changing the engine oil often enough, thus allowing the hydraulic lifters (which are located between the camshaft and the pushrods) to gum up. This will preclude proper adjustment.

It might be possible to correct the condition by adjusting the play between the pushrods and rocker arms per instructions in an AMC service manual. If not, the chances are you'll have to have the lifters replaced.

I recently bought a brand new large car (I'd rather not disclose the brand), and after 450 miles transmission trouble developed—it wouldn't shift out of low gear.

By the time it reached 3,361 miles, this had happened seven times, with the car overheating considerably each time. The transmission problem now seems corrected after four trips to the garage.

Now, at 4,500 miles, the car has used nine quarts of oil. Even though the engine now runs fairly smoothly, it still burns oil excessively. I am told that this may correct itself after another 2,000 or 3,000 miles. Might it burn even more oil at 20,000 or 30,000 miles?

What can I do?

The first thing is to try to get some action from your dealer while the car is still under warranty because you're sure to at least have your current problem indefinitely.

Whoever told you the oil consumption problem might work itself out is looking for a certified miracle.

There's no doubt in my mind that the excessive overheating has resulted in excessive wear inside the engine, and that is what is causing the

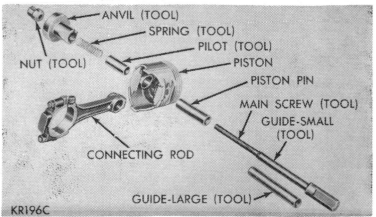

Fig. 3-5. Fitting of the wristpin (or piston pin) must be perfect. If it works loose, protrusion can ruin the engine. (Courtesy Chrysler Corp.)

29

oil consumption. Chances are this wear is limited to the cylinder walls, and it conceivably could be corrected by reboring the cylinders and using a set of oversized pistons.

If it were my car and I could document beyond doubt that the problem was caused by the defective transmission, I would insist on at least having a new shortblock installed. A shortblock includes the basic engine block and internal pieces.

If you are unable to get satisfaction from the dealer, send a certified letter (so you have proof of contact) to the manufacturer's local zone office detailing all the problems and listing the current status, including mileage. If for some reason the zone doesn't satisfy you, follow the same procedure to the manufacturer's home office.

I just bought a 1965 Rambler Ambassador with six-cylinder engine. The man who sold it to me said I would get 18 miles to the gallon and add oil about once a month. I don't get the 18 miles to the gallon and must add about a quart of oil a week.

I went back the man's house, but it was empty. The people next door told me that he had moved out of state. Do you have any suggestions, especially about the oil consumption?

Presumably you never studied Latin. If you had, caveat emptor (let the buyer beware) might have stuck in your mind. You were, as they say, ripped off. As for the oil problem, your engine certainly has internal problems. In lieu of an expensive overhaul, you might try a can or two of a heavy oil additive. These products thicken the oil and thus reduce consumption.

We have a 1969 Lincoln Continental that has overheated from a broken hose. We replaced the hoses and put in new coolant. We also put in new oil, and that is where our problem lies. When started from cold, the oil pressure gauge reads full (high), but as the motor heats up, the needle drops to no reading at all. Does this car take a special oil or should we drain all the oil and start over?

The car does not run hot—the needle is always a little below the center mark on the temperature gauge. Our mechanics are baffled by this.

It may be that your mechanics are baffled because they like you too much to give you the bad news. I suspect that when the hose went and you continued to operate the car, it overheated to such an extent that serious internal engine problems developed. And continuing to run it without oil pressure will make things worse.

If you want to avoid the expense—upwards of $500 or more—of tearing the engine down to discover the problem and fix it, you might keep body and soul together by adding a can (probably two) of one of the many thick oil additives on the market. Unless things are really shot or the oil pump is failing, this should bring your oil pressure back. One word of caution, thickening the oil this way can make the engine hard to start in very cold weather.

I have a 1975 Ford Maverick with a 250-cubic-inch, six-cylinder engine. Recently, with just under 20,000 miles on it, I took the car in for a tune-up. The mechanic did a compression check and discovered that there is low compression in two cylinders.

I was informed that this was caused by bad valve guides that did not allow the valves to seat properly, allowing carbon to build up and compression to decline. The mechanic said there has been a lot of trouble with valve guides in the 250 engines, but a person at the dealer's shop said he had never heard of such problems.

If the problem does exist, could you furnish some statistics?

Obviously, the problem does exist. You have it. As for being inherent in the 250 six, I don't think so. That engine has been in production for several years, and any widespread problem such as you describe would have shown up and been corrected long before your car was manufactured.

This is not to say that others might not also have the same problem. I just don't believe it is as widespread as you are being led to believe. Conversely, I'm sure it isn't as rare as your dealer's representative says.

Your course of action is obvious. The simplest and best (but not cheapest) remedy is to have your mechanic or a good machine shop do a complete valve job. It should cost less than $100, plus the cost of the labor to remove and reinstall the head.

Chapter 4
Fuel Systems

I presently own a 1976 Pinto (2,300 cc engine), a car that I am rather pleased with. However, since I have moved to a rather sandy environment, I have found a problem in the air cleaner system.

It seems that particles of sand are occasionally being drawn under the air cleaner element. I find them under the filter and within its perimeter and presume they are being drawn into the carburetor. Neither the brand of air cleaner nor tightness of cover make a difference.

A local dealer says he finds the problem in many cars and knows of nothing to be done about it. He also doesn't consider it a cause for concern. What's your opinion?

If it were my car, I would be concerned to the point of getting something done to it. After all, what is an air cleaner for if not to keep foreign particles from entering the engine. And anything as big as a grain of sand is big enough to cause a problem.

If the dealer can't or won't do anything, I would contact the customer relations person at the local Ford zone office and explain it to him. If you don't have success there, contact Ford Consumer Office in Dearborn, Mich. There undoubtedly is an answer, and you should find it before any serious damage is done.

You might make sure that you are using the correct element. Since Pintos have used only the 2,300 four-cylinder engine for the last three years, I doubt if there's been a mix-up, but it's possible.

And, although all major-brand after-market products are made to exacting factory specifications, there's a remote possibility that somebody goofed. If you haven't already tried a Ford Motorcraft filter, you should. If you still have trouble, that would be further ammunition for your cause.

I have a 1976 six-cylinder Ford Granada with 9,500 miles on it. The car usually starts out with a normal idle but, after driving

15 miles or so, the idle goes crazy and the car chokes out. I wait a few seconds and the car starts again, idling very rough. It does this every time I slow down. The garage says everything is set right—timing, carburetor, etc. But it still stalls and runs rough. Any ideas?

It would seem you have trouble with the carburetor choke—either the butterfly valve is sticking or the automatic heat sensor is malfunctioning. What this does is cause a very rich mixture to flow into the engine. This is desirable when the engine is cold. But as it warms up, it has a tendency to flood, fouling the plugs.

The next time it happens, open the hood and remove the air cleaner. If the butterfly (a flat piece of metal up to two inches in diameter) is horizontal, push the rear of it down. It should stay open and the car should run. You might try lubricating the shaft that runs across the center of the butterfly and into the carburetor housing. If this doesn't fix it, have the garage check the choke heat sensor and replace if necessary.

I recently purchased a 1973 Chevrolet. My only complaint is that it constantly throws out black smoke from the exhaust. I've tried all kinds of gasoline—high test, regular, and unleaded. Any ideas?

Black exhaust is indicative of a too-rich fuel-air mixture—you're burning too much fuel. I recommend a tune-up, at the very least a carburetor adjustment. By the way, your car was intended to run on regular gas.

My brother has a 1967 Toronado. He has a hard time starting it and when he starts to drive, the whole front end shakes. He put in new spark plugs. He took them out a week later and they were black with dirt. He put in another set and when he took these out, they were clean. What could be wrong?

It sounds like your brother's car is in need of a major tune-up with some special attention being paid to the carburetor. When spark plugs foul, it is indicative of an air-to-fuel mixture that is far too rich (that is, too much gasoline). What happens is that the mixture does not burn completely and the resultant residue collects on all areas of the combustion chamber. Then after the car is driven awhile, this buildup impedes the function of the plugs and the car begins to run rough, often shaking violently.

I am a bit confused when you say a second set of plugs were clean, but that could be because the car wasn't driven enough to allow the buildup.

There is one other possibility if the black substance on the plugs is oily: it would indicate deterioration of the rings or valve seals which would require a hotter firing plug in lieu of a major engine overhaul.

I have a 1975 Saab EMS with 29,000 miles on it. Since purchasing it about a year ago, the engine has been making a sound similar to backfire (only from the engine compartment) when the accelerator is depressed during shifting. This occurs when the engine is cold and sometimes after being parked only two hours.

Recently, it was given a complete tune-up , and an "enrichment kit" was installed per Saab instructions to the dealer. Since then this popping or knocking sound has been occurring more frequently. When in fourth gear, it runs smoothly. What could be the problem?

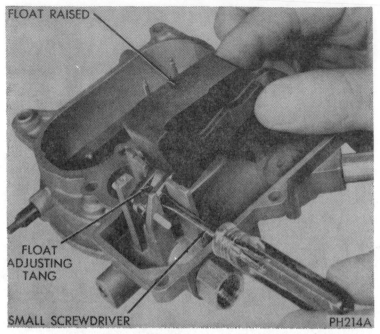

FLOAT RAISED

FLOAT
ADJUSTING
TANG

SMALL SCREWDRIVER   PH214A

Fig. 4-1. Adjustment of the carburetor float is critical. This float determines the amount of fuel in the chamber. (Courtesy Chrysler Corp.)

The early 1975 Saabs with the new fuel injection system had the problem you describe. According to a Saab engineer, your engine is running a little on the lean side and you're getting a backfire through the injection system.

The problem, he thinks, is that when your dealer installed the enrichment kit, which acts much in the manner of an automatic choke, he did not install a warm-up regulator and a new thermal time switch, which operates the system for 45 seconds instead of the normal 30.

The people at Saab say this entire modification is covered under your warranty.

I have a 1973 Cutlass Supreme with a 350 engine and four-barrel carburetor. It runs well on level roads but when I go up a long incline, it bucks and hesitates, but keeps going. I have had two complete tune-ups and mentioned this to the mechanic, but no one seems to know what causes this condition. I use a good grade of regular gasoline. Kindly advise.

Although you have had the car tuned, I would recheck both the condition and gap of the spark plugs. The reason for this is that even one plug in poor condition will cause these symptoms, especially under a heavier than normal load such as climbing a grade. If the plugs check out OK, the next most likely candidate is the float chamber in the carburetor. If the float (Fig. 4-1) is not set to the exact recommended angle, the level of fuel in the chamber could be low enough to provide an adequate fuel supply in level and downhill conditions but starve the engine and cause it to cut out going up hills. And while you're under the hood, take an air hose and blow out the radiator core from the back. It's remotely possible that debris in the core could reduce the cooling function enough that, under load conditions, the engine could overheat sufficiently to cause your problems.

I have a 1969 Ford LTD with a 302 engine and I've had trouble with it in cold weather. In the morning, I start it up, let it stand to warm up, then take off for work. Every time I come to a stop sign or a light, it'll stall as soon as I take off again unless I take my foot off the gas pedal and step on it again. It even does it after slowing down for a corner and getting back on the gas.

I put in new spark plugs, new points, new rotor, new condenser, new fuel filter, new distributor cap, new PCV valve, all new ignition wires, and a rebuilt carburetor. I even changed the choke setting and richened the fuel mixture and it still does it. Do you have any suggestions?

There are three possible areas of solution—fuel system, ignition system, and valves. Although you have touched on many probable causes, and some not so probable, I will list the most likely candidates.

In the fuel system, possibilities include wrong idle (Fig. 4-2) or mixture adjustment (by changing these you might have aggravated the situation), improper choke operation, incorrect carburetor float setting, defective fuel pump, or dirt and/or water in the fuel system.

In the ignition, it can be bad or improperly adjusted points, a defective coil or condensor, a worn distributor rotor, or defective ignition wiring.

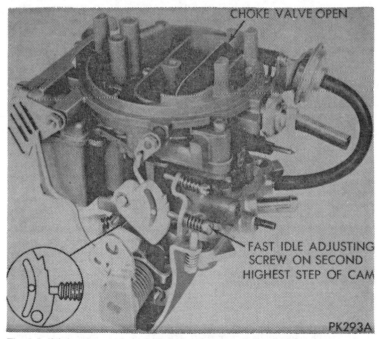

Fig. 4-2. If the carburetor's fast-idle adjustment is off, the engine will run too fast or too slow, the latter causing stalling. (Courtesy Chrysler Corp.)

With valves, it may be a matter of misadjustment. If there is insufficient lash, it does not permit the valves to open the proper time or distance, reducing the amount of fuel mixture in the cylinders.

I have a 1963 Dodge 440 that had been getting about 12 miles to the gallon of gas. The mechanic I deal with said if I'd get a tune-up my mileage would increase so I agreed.

Now my mileage is between 7.5 and 8.5 miles per gallon. He changed my carburetor three times (no charge) and still no increase in mileage. The last time, he gave it a compression check and that was okay. Do you have any ideas?

There are several possibilities but I'd first like to say that 12 miles per gallon isn't that far out of line for a car of that vintage with an engine that big. The only time you're going to get better mileage from a tune-up is when the car is out of tune to start with.

Back to your problem. Assuming your tune-up included properly gapped and properly installed spark plugs and breaker points and a check of the timing, the chances are that your problem still lies in the carburetor.

The probabilities include the float valve set too high, the needle valve not closing fully on its seat, fuel mixture too rich, the power valve not operating properly or the jets worn or the wrong size. It could also be a defective choke.

Other possibilities include a partially clogged air cleaner that would restrict the flow of air and automatically richen the mixture, excessive rolling resistance that could be caused by dragging brakes, tight bearings, abnormally low tire pressure, or misalignment of the front end.

I have a new carburetor on my 1968 Valiant. It starts very well when the engine is cold but when it is hot and I try to start it, I have trouble.

There are times when it starts right away, but there are many times when I just keep grinding away. It is like a toothache. When the mechanic looks at it, it works fine. Can you give me any suggestions as to why it would work like that?

Generally speaking, there are two reasons why a car is hard to start when hot. Most likely there are fuel system problems, such as partial clogging of fuel lines or filters, the choke sticking shut or being totally inoperative, carburetor float valve sticking, improper idle speed or mixture adjustment, faulty fuel pump, air leaks, or vapor lock.

Less likely, but still a possibility is low engine compression that could be caused by a leaky head gasket, worn piston rings, out-of-round cylinders, burned or sticking valves, improper valve adjustment, or loss of vacuum at intake manifold.

I have a 1971 Plymouth Custom sedan with an eight-cylinder engine, four-barrel carburetor. I cannot understand why I am using so much gasoline. I had the carburetor overhauled twice to no avail. I was told to put a two-barrel carburetor on the car, necessitating an adapter plate. Now the car hood won't close. I have to reroute the fuel line and get a different linkage setup. Can you give me any information on this problem?

For starters, I would go back to the four-barrel carburetor—it is a lot simpler. In the same kind of application, a two-barrel has larger venturis than the four barrel and uses as much, if not more, gasoline. In virtually all

PP72

Fig. 4-3. Through the use of various diagnostic equipment, technicians can tune your carburetor for optimum performance and fuel mileage. (Courtesy Chrysler Corp.)

four-barrel setups, the engine runs most of the time on two barrels. The other two provide extra power when the accelerator pedal is floored. Some people try to cut down on their fuel consumption by disconnecting the supplementary barrels (usually toward the rear). But the saving in fuel usually is more than offset by the loss in performance.

After replacing the four-barrel carburetor, take the car to a diagnostic service center where, through the use of various machines, a technician can adjust your carburetor (Fig. 4-3) for maximum economy and performance. After that, keep a close watch on your driving style, which plays a major role in fuel economy or lack thereof.

I would like to know if there is a cure for carburetor icing on my 1968 Dodge Coronet with a 225 cubic inch six-cylinder engine, automatic transmission, and power steering. I recently installed a new carburetor but the problem persists, stalling during very damp or rainy weather prior to engine warmup. Ice and moisture are visible on the carburetor during stallout. The fast and slow idles are set to specifications, and the ignition and manifold heat valve are in excellent condition.

The overwhelming majority of cases like yours are caused by manifold heat valve (Fig. 4-4) that isn't functioning properly. It must be clean, and operating freely at all times. If, as you say, your valve is in good order, the only other problem I can suggest is the fuel mixture. You say the fast and

37

slow idles are set to specs, but if the mixture is just the slightest bit on the lean side (more air, less fuel) than required, it can cause icing.

I have a 1974 Plymouth Voyager Sport Van with a 318 cubic inch V-8 engine. My problem is that while driving along, the engine will just shut off without any warning. If I wait five or six hours, it starts. My garage has tried everything from replacing all the electronic equipment to new gasoline filters. Within a week, it starts doing the same thing again. It's gotten to the point that I'm afraid to drive it very far. I've contacted Chrysler, both in Detroit and locally, and they've offered no help. Any suggestions?

My first thought is the ignition coil, but since you've had that replaced to no avail, I would recommend a change in the distributor condensor. It's unusual, but they can be adversely affected by heat to the point that they don't store up a big enough charge to enable the plugs to ignite the fuel-air mixture.

Another possibility, also remote, is vapor lock. It's entirely possible that a fuel line is routed too close to the engine block and it's allowing vapor lock to develop. A third possibility is a minute crack in the fuel pump diaphragm that might expand enough to drop pressure to a point where it won't properly fuel the engine. To determine whether it's fuel or ignition trouble, disconnect the fuel line at the carburetor immediately after the problem develops. Take care—that engine's hot. Then, with the coil wire removed, crank the engine. If fuel spurts out, the problem is ignition.

Lastly, you might want to make sure the fuel tank (or cap) is properly vented. If not, it will create a vacuum that will overcome the pressure of the fuel pump and halt the flow.

Fig. 4-4. The heat valve, located at the bottom of the manifold, must be clean and moving freely. (Courtesy Chrysler Corp.)

I have a 1972 Chevrolet with a 6-cylinder engine that has a stalling problem, particularly after it sits for a few hours. It happens on July 4 or Dec. 25 so it can't be the weather. One day after sitting idle for two hours, it stalled three times. I have stalled on trolley tracks and going around corners. Can you advise?

My first inclination is to think that your idle speed adjustment is set too low. At warm idle in neutral, the average car should run at about 700-800 revolutions per minute. If it idles at less than that, especially in an automatic-transmission equipped vehicle, it becomes critical. The shift into any gear often is enough to cause stalling. This would also show up in turns where you get off the gas and the engine downshifts. If the engine idle speed turns out all right, you might take a close look at the automatic choke. If it isn't functioning right, it could definitely be a contributing factor.

I have a 1974 Plymouth Sebring and just had a new choke assembly installed. When the car is started after being in a closed garage all night, it seems to choke up a little. In rainy weather, the car starts, but when I put it in drive it stalls. This goes on for several minutes and after many starts and a warm-up period, it finally goes. What can be wrong and what should be done?

Chances are you have a jammed heat-riser on the engine's exhaust manifold. This is a valve-type device that is actuated by extremes of temperature. Its purpose is to pre-heat the flow of air to the carburetor when the engine is cold and to assist in the engine warming process by impeding the flow of exhaust gasses. Many times this device rusts to the point where it jams open, allowing cold air to reach the carburetor.

I have a 1976 Ford Pinto with a 2,300-cc engine, automatic transmission, and electronic ignition. In starting when temperature is below 20 degrees, the engine fires quickly but stalls before reaching fast idle. If the temperature is 10 degrees or below, I have to start the engine three times before it will continue to run. If a fourth start is needed, the battery does not have enough cranking power to turn the engine. My dealer says the engine is set to specifications. The engine starts perfectly when warm. What can be the problem?

My first inclination would be to fault the automatic choke mechanism, but if your dealer's mechanic really has checked to see that all adjustments are set to specifications, the only other likely culprit is the gasoline you are using. Any water that gets into the gasoline will freeze when it gets down in the temperature range you talk about. Although it's hardly a problem in warm weather. I would suggest you try a can of dry-gas (there are several brands on the market) when the temperatures fall later in the year. As a back-up, I also would keep a can of ether handy for quick starts in extreme cold.

I have a 1970 Jaguar XKE roadster which has a normal idle speed of 750 revolutions per minute. After idling a few minutes, the rmp zooms up to about 1,500. I have a shop manual for the car, but it shows nothing for this problem. Can you offer any suggestions?

Assuming this happens when the engine is both warm and cold, I would say it is what's known as carburetor surge. This is usually caused by a malfunction of the dashpots, but the best way to make sure the job is corrected is to buy rebuild kits (probably available only through your dealer) and carefully rebuild each carburetor. When you reinstall them, make sure they are properly calibrated and balanced. If the problem only shows up when the engine is cold, it definitely is related to the choke mechanism, which I am sure your manual covers.

After stopping my car at an intersection, when I start again it stalls. In order to restart the engine I have to feed it very little gas and sometimes this fails. Also, aren't the alternators on the new cars the same as generators on older cars?

Your stalling problem sounds very much like carburetor trouble, most likely in the setting of the automatic choke. This can cause an overly rich fuel-air mixture that, in effect, floods the engine. It also will result in poor fuel economy.

You are correct in that alternators and generators serve the same purpose—that of supplying electrical power. They do it in entirely different ways, however. A generator is a direct current (DC) producer and the engine actually draws battery power at idle speed. An alternator works on alternating current (AC) and continually provides electricity. The alternator is a much more efficient unit.

My 1969 Chyrsler has 12,900 miles on it. It has new plugs, points, and condenser and never has been driven hard. Could you please tell me why it stalls at a light or when it is idling. Then I have to start it a dozen times before I get started again. It has always started well, except these spells.

I have had additives put in the gas tank and also had the carburetor and choke cleaned. Also the manifold heat control valve is kept free.

When you say the car has always started well "except these spells," it leads me to think you might occasionally be picking up a tank of contaminated gasoline. This can happen, especially in older installations, when a station's inground tanks get old and split, permitting either water or dirt to mix with the gasoline. It also happens at stations where there is a relatively small turnover of products. If either of these situations could apply to you, try filling up elsewhere for awhile to see if the problem goes away.

If that does not prove to be the case, there are other things you might check. First, if you have not replaced (or cleaned in the case of a permanent installation) the car's fuel filter recently, do so because it can be clogged just enough to cause sporadic problems.

Although you have had both the carb and choke cleaned, it is possible that enough "varnish" has built up in critical areas to impede fuel flow. Also, in having the carb cleaned, it is possible that the float angle was changed, resulting in too much or too little fuel, causing stalling.

I have a 1966 Rambler with six-cylinder engine. When I start the car from cold, it idles perfectly until the automatic choke cuts off. Then it idles very rough unless I put it in neutral, when it stops shaking and smoothes out.

I've had several opinions. One mechanic said I need a new carburetor; another said it was timing; another said I need a valve job. I've had it tuned up, but it still shakes. Otherwise it runs fine. Any suggestions?

There are several possibilites. Probably your trouble is caused by improper idle mixture adjustment, idle speed, or both. It could be compounded by a dirty carburetor. If this is what it turns out to be and the price is right, you might be advised to have a rebuilt carburetor installed.

Other possibilities include air leaks in the fuel intake system, a sticking heat control valve on the manifold, and various ignition problems such as insufficient point gap, defective coil, bad condenser rotor, cracked cap, worn plugs, or faulty wiring.

Take the car to a reputable shop that specializes in complete diagnostic checks and it will be able to determine electronically where the problem lies.

Last June, I bought a Buick Skylark with a V-6 engine. Current mileage is 4,500. The engine dies on me (starting from cold) at two consecutive stop signs within a block. Keeping a foot on the gas pedal is the only way to keep it running.

When I come to a full stop, the car vibrates. If I keep my foot on the gas, I can totally eliminate the vibrations. I've had it back for service and they adjust the idle to no avail. Any suggestions?

To most people, adjusting the idle means a simple movement of a screw on the throttle linkage to increase or decrease the speed at which the engine runs with no pressure on the accelerator pedal.

There is another adjustment called idle fuel mixture which, if it isn't set properly, can cause all the symptoms that you describe. It is adjusted by one or more screws (depending on the number of carburetor barrels in specific applications) located near the base of the carburetor.

A rule of thumb for years has been to turn the screw clockwise until it is all the way in, then back it out a turn and a half. But with today's more sophisticated systems, that should be used only in an emergency and the adjustment should be made by a qualified technician with the proper diagnostic equipment.

Although I believe that is where your problem lies, there are numerous other possibilities that singly or in groups could cause your troubles. Some of those possibilities include dirt or water in the fuel filter, defective or misadjusted automatic choke, leaks in the carburetor or intake manifold gaskets, defective fuel pump, worn or damaged carburetor metering jet, or other internal carburetor problems.

Chapter 5
Ignition

Of all the automotive problems asked about, the most prevalent is that of dieseling or post ignition in which the car's engine continues to run after the ignition is turned off. Running a close second is that of engine pinging, a situation that occurs most often with leaded gasoline.

In all models since 1975, these problems can be interrelated and, in many cases, can't be entirely solved. I will try to explain both situations.

Dieseling is caused by a buildup of foreign material inside the combustion chamber. These deposits become extremely hot and act like substitute spark plugs when the ignition is turned off. The engine, therefore, keeps running, albeit roughly.

This problem is more likely to occur in cars running on leaded gasoline in the lower octane ranges, although it has become a factor in some newer cars using unleaded gas.

It is more often a factor in cars used for short trips or at relatively low speeds. This is because the engine never is run hard enough to clean out these deposits.

The best solution to dieseling is to buy a tankful of the highest available octane gas—be it leaded or unleaded, add a can of gasoline additive, and drive the car on an interstate highway at 50 miles per hour in second gear for five minutes or so. For cars with a two-speed automatic, you can get the same result by running at 35 mph in low for the same period of time. This will be enough, in 95 percent of the cases, to clear up the dieseling effect. The others will require the removal and cleaning of the cylinder heads.

The pinging that is showing up in some 1975 and 1976 models is technically known as pre-ignition. That is, the fuel is firing under compression before the spark plug ignites.

It is caused by two things. If the octane level of the fuel is not high enough, it will explode under pressure. If the timing is retarded, the spark itself will be late.

There have been some isolated instances in which late model cars are stricken with both maladies, usually after 10,000 miles or so. It can be cured only by "blowing out" the deposits that cause the dieseling and then having the timing set and maintained exactly to specifications. Some cars also require premimum unleaded fuel, which is not sold by all stations.

Under no circumstances can either pre-ignition or post-ignition be considered normal or harmless. Pre-ignition can lead eventually to serious valve and or piston damage—an expansive repair job. Post-ignition puts excess strain on many components, and premature engine failure may result.

I have a problem that is not unique—dieseling, or post ignition, of my car's engine. I have tried everything—just had it tuned three months ago, even tried a tank of high-test gasoline on the advice of several people. The car is a 1973 Dodge Dart with a 225 cubic inch, six-cylinder engine. Is there a cure?

The trouble you describe—that of the engine continuing to "run" after the key has been shut off—is a direct result of efforts by the manufacturers to meet federal emission standards through the process of detuning the engine. Since the introduction of the catalytic converter on 1975 models, dieseling has become much less a factor. But that's of little solace to you.

The problem of dieseling becomes much more of a factor when a car is used exclusively or almost exclusively for short, relatively low-speed operations. This permits the buildup of carbon deposits in the combustion chamber which remain hot enough to keep igniting the fuel after the ignition key is turned off.

There are several gasoline additives on the market (Wynn's, Bardahl, STP, etc.) which in many cases can burn out these carbon deposits. The best application is to pour a can down through the carburetor with the engine running, then add a can or two to a tankful of gasoline.

Another way of stopping post-ignition is to depress the accelerator pedal to the floor immediately after turning off the key. This, in effect, will flood the chambers and eliminate the dieseling. Repeated use of this procedure could cause excessive wear because the flood of gas will wash the lubricating oil from the walls of the cylinders and eventually contaminate the oil in the sump.

Another often-proposed but highly ill-advised method is to shut the engine off with the car in gear to let the drive train absorb the shock. This puts undue strain on such items as the transmission, universal joints, and ring and pinion.

I have a 1976 El Camino that has a pinging noise everytime I take off from a standing start. I've taken it to the dealer twice and had the mechanic drive it. They tell me it is octane ping and there is nothing they can do about it. Isn't there something that can be done?

You and many others are caught in the middle of a situation that is, at best, confusing. First let me say that in all probability the mechanic is right. The pinging you get on acceleration is technically known as pre-ignition. Generally it is caused by the air fuel mixture exploding in the combustion chamber under compression rather than at the point of plug fire.

Briefly, what you need is a higher octane rated gasoline. But that is not as simple as it may seem. There are two ways of rating the octane of gasoline—called research and motor. Since they are done by different processes, you can find that fuels with ratings of 87 to 91 can be the same. Generally, an average of the two ratings is used on the pump—say 89.

Many owners of cars requiring unleaded gasoline are finding that this 89 octane fuel isn't good enough. Some oil companies, therefore, are making a higher grade unleaded. This should be clearly marked on the station pumps.

If you shop around and find a station that offers unleaded gas with an octane rating in the 90s, you should cure the pinging.

I have a 1973 Gran Torino with 26,000 miles on it. I bought it new and have had a ping in the motor under heavy load ever since. I have had the timing checked several times, and the Ford mechanics say it is on the button. They say if they change the timing I would lose power.

I have always used 90 or better octane gasoline in the 351-cubic-inch motor. Do you have any ideas?

Slightly retarded timing is most often the cause of pinging in these circumstances, but since your dealer has checked it more than once and the problem continues, there are a few other areas that you might look at.

If it is pinging (pre-ignition) and not knocking (detonation), there are four distinct possibilities, only one of which is relatively simple (and inexpensive) to cure. We'll start there. Spark plugs of too high a heat range or plugs with broken or cracked insulators can cause pinging.

Another possibility is combustion chamber carbon deposits that remain incandescent and thereby fire the mixture prematurely. (This often is accompanied by post-ignition, in which the engine diesels after the ignition is shut off.) Usual cause here is a preponderance of low-speed, short trip operation.

Then there is excessive heat in the combustion chamber such as hot spots caused by poor cooling in the jacket area around the valves. Last, the valves themselves can be too hot.

If it's detonation, the cause can be something as simple as running the fuel mixture too lean or using fuel of too low an octane rating.

I have a 1975 Mercury Monarch with automatic transmission and 6-cylinder engine. It also has electronic ignition. If it rains all day, the car will not start. I have sprayed it and used dry gas but neither works. When the weather is dry, it is okay. Do you have any suggestions?

Despite the fact that yours isn't the only complaint I've had along these lines, the engineers at Ford say they know of no particular trend toward damp hard starting. Those engineers say that your problem can not be in any way related to the solid-state ignition system; therefore, it must be a problem with the carburetion.

The most likely candidate is the automatic choke. If it is sticking, it will very quickly flood the engine and prevent starting. Neither the people at Ford nor I can understand why your dealer has been unable to fix your problem.

Give the shop another chance, and if it's still not repaired to your satisfaction, contact the owner relations office in your area (it's in the telephone book under Ford Motor Co.) and explain the situation to them in as reasonable a manner as possible. They will arrange for a service engineer to go over the car at your dealer's shop.

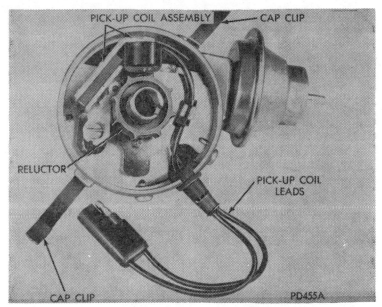

Fig. 5-1. The heart of the solid state ignition system is the electronic distributor which is free of breaker points. (Courtesy Chrysler Corp.)

I would like to know if I can convert the ignition system on my 1971 Pinto from the conventional system to the new solid-state type of ignition. If so, how much should it cost?

I have seen several conversion kits offered on the "universal" type which means they can be adapted for use on various types and models of cars. They usually go in the range of $50. If you are going to have it installed, it'll probably cost you as much as $15 more. Ford offers a conversion kit for all American cars except four-cylinder models (which excluded your Pinto) under its Motorcraft parts label. There is one major advantage of the solid-state electronic ignition systems that are standard on all American-made cars now: since there are no points or condenser (Fig. 5-1) to wear out and no mechanical wear for the sensor and trigger wheel, the timing and dwell will remain constant for the life of the system.

I have a 1975 Ford with solid-state ignition system. I would like to know if, because of the catalytic converter, I must take the car to my dealer for an engine tune-up or can any reputable shop handle the job?

I am not sure I understand the reasoning beind your question, but I will say right off that the type of ignition system has no bearing on the catalytic converter. As to tune-ups, any reputable shop has a list of specifications to which your ignition and carburetion should be set and should be able to handle the job.

I have a 1974 Pontiac Bonneville with a 400-cubic-inch V-8 engine, four-barrel carburetor, and high-energy ignition. No service manual lists tune-up specifications for a 1974 Pontiac with the high-energy ignition. In 1975, when that ignition became standard, the specifications changed. Would I get better performance by advancing the timing and using spark plugs with a wider gap as stipulated in the 1975 specs?

The tune-up specifications for your car—as with any General Motors product of recent vintage—are printed on a label located on the radiator shroud under your hood. You should not vary from these instructions to any significant degree because you could cause permanent (and expensive) engine problems. For instance, a 4-degree advance in the timing could lead to a burned piston, burned valves, or both.

There also is the distinct likelihood of throwing the car's emission system out of kilter which, in many cases, can cause the engine to perform worse than it did before.

If for some reason the spec sheet is not pasted on the radiator shroud—it could have been washed away in steam cleaning—the service department of any Pontiac dealer will have a book listing specs for all recent engines.

I have a 1973 Impala which will not start in the rain. When I replaced the distributor cap, it made no difference. The car will start, however, if the engine is warm, no matter what the weather. Where could the problem lie?

The great majority of problems in this area are caused by a breakdown in the insulation of the ignition wiring—the thick black wires that run from your distributor to the various spark plugs and the coil. If it isn't the wires, chances are you have a breakdown of the insulation in the coil. If you haven't had it done lately, I would strongly recommend a general tune-up (on diagnostic machinery) which should reveal and cure the problem as well as improving the car's basic performance and economy.

I have a 1971 Peugeot 304 that is difficult to start on foggy days when moisture collects on the various parts under the hood. I have sprayed all wiring with waterproofing material to no avail. The only way I have solved the problem is by using an old hair drier to blow heated air over the various ignition components. Sometimes this is not feasible and I am stuck for hours until old mother nature dries things out. Do you have any suggestions?

You obviously have an insulation breakdown on one or more parts of the ignition system, and you'll have to make several checks and—possibly—replace items in a hit-or-miss process until you find the trouble. The waterproofing spray you speak of is usually a complete waste of money. The only way these products can be of help is if each part to be sealed is removed, cleaned thoroughly and sprayed from all angles. Even then, such a thing as a cracked distributor cap or a split wire will continue to cause trouble in high-humidity situations. The most likely cause of your trouble is breakdown of the high-voltage ignition wires. To check, lift the hood while it's running at night and if you see sparks jumping all about, the wires should be replaced. If the problem persists, you'll have to throughly check both the distributor cap and the coil for leakage.

I have a 1972 Toyota Corolla with 42,000 miles. It is, basically, a decent automobile and gets fairly good mileage. However, there is a problem of condensation in the distributor cap and air filter which builds up whenever we have more than a slight rainstorm.

I have had the electrical wires replaced three time, have had high-powered spark plugs put in, but nothing alleviates the problem. Each time it happens, the tow truck must come to get me started. Can you offer any suggestions, short of buying the garage?

You have hit on the problem without realizing the solution. The buildup of condensation in the distributor cap is what's causing your trouble. When this happens, it short-circuits the high voltage to ground rather than out through the wires to the spark plugs.

The cause is something else again. Obviously, it is a result of a leak in the distributor big enough to permit dampness to enter. Chances are that a crack or chip in the distributor cap is the culprit, as is the case 95 percent of the time.

If you replace the cap and that doesn't solve it, enlist the aid of a friend the next time it happens and check to see if there is a healthy spark by positioning the end of the wire a quarter inch away from the top of the plug while the engine is being cranked. Wear heavy gloves to avoid a shock.

If you get no spark at the plug, try the heavy coil that goes into the distributor from the coil. If no spark is there, use a 12-volt test lamp to see if juice is getting in and out of the low-voltage coil wires. If the bulb lights, chances are good you have a bad coil. One possibility there is that improperly gapped plugs could short out the whole system. A simple resetting would solve that problem.

I have a 1973 Grand Prix. The problem is in starting the car after it is hot.

I have installed three starters and one battery in the last six months. I am told that the problem exists in many cars with large engines. I'm told that the engine parts (piston, etc.) expand when hot, making the engine too tight to turn over. I have found that after a 5 or 10 minute wait, the engine will turn over and start. I might add that the present starter in the car is a high-torque starter. Same problem.

I would appreciate any comments or suggestions you might have.

It is true that the heat that builds up inside of an internal combustion engine will cause parts to expand. But the heat should not be so great as to cause the engine to virtually seize.

I would suggest the following. First, make sure your engine timing is exactly right. If the timing is off to any degree, especially if retarded, it will cause the engine to run hotter than it should and might cause excessive internal expansion.

Second, I would make sure the cooling system is clean and free flowing and that the thermostat is operating properly. To check the thermostat, heat water to its operating temperature (stamped on the thermostat) and drop it in. The thermostat should open and, when removed, close. You might even try a lower temperature unit.

Third, and perhaps most important, check the condition of your engine crankcase oil. Excessive heat will cause the lubricating qualities of the oil to break down sooner, and that will increase the friction, causing even more heat.

During the past few weeks, my car has been running very sluggishly. It is very hard to start, especially in the mornings. Lately, it has started to backfire through the exhaust system and carburetor. The car has about 118,000 miles on it. What do you think could be wrong? Is it expensive?

It sounds very much like one of two things. Either your engine is in dire need of a general tune-up (especially the timing) or a valve job. I would start by having the timing reset and, if that doesn't cure it, have it tuned up—both are relatively inexpensive. If it's still not right, chances are you need a fairly expensive valve job, which might not be feasible on a car with such high mileage.

A couple years ago, I bought a 1968 Plymouth with a 383-cubic-inch V-8 engine and automatic transmission. Specs show timing to be 7 1/2 degrees before top dead center and firing order is 1-8-4-3-6-5-7-2. When I attempted to time the engine, I couldn't find the timing mark at all when wired to the number one plug. I aligned the timing marks and found the rotor pointed to the number-six plug. What could they have done to cause this?

Assuming you are on the correct plug (number one is at the left front of the engine), the only other explanation is that at some time in the past someone removed the distributor and replaced it 180 degrees out of phase. This would make the engine impossible to time accurately. It could only be done by ear, which involves loosening the retaining screw, turning the distributor to the left until it stalls, turning it to the right until it stalls, then tightening it up as close to the middle as possible.

Chapter 6
Electrical Systems

I have a 1970 Mustang Mach I with a 351 Cleveland engine. After running at operating temperature and then being stopped, the car will not start for an hour or so. It reacts as if the battery is dead. The engine will not turn. Also, if allowed to idle for 5 or 10 minutes, the engine overheats, with or without a thermostat. The engine has been tuned, the timing was checked, a new battery and starter was installed, and the cooling system and radiator was thoroughly cleaned. Any clues?

Since I've seen this starting problem happening many times—including to myself as recently as the last year—I'd be willing to bet that the problem is with your new battery. All batteries are not the same, even though they may look identical. The bargain you get on a battery, especially where you are using it on a larger engine, often turns into a headache and, eventually, a liability. The secret is in cranking power, which is determined by the number of plates in a battery. Many cars, especially big-engined Fords, require considerably more cranking power when they are hot than cold. In the same area, make sure that all wiring connections are both clean and tight and the wires themselves are in good condition. Often, deterioration at the point where the battery cables join the clamps can be enough to impede the flow of electricity.

I have a 1970 Cadillac with 50,000 miles on it. When cold, it will start very easily. But when hot, it gets cantankerous, as though it had a weak battery. I also replaced the battery wires and voltage regulator and had the alternator checked out. The timing also was checked. Nothing seems to help. Do you have any suggestions?

In some instances owners have done all the above and also replaced the starter. This problem can be traced to the battery, the starter, or the wires and their connections, assuming the car starts normally under other than hot conditions.

The usual villain is the battery. Either it is too old to provide the extra punch to turn things over when hot or it is a cut-rate unit that doesn't have the necessary plates and therefore the cranking power.

Occasionally the problem can be traced to the starter when, due to the excessive heat of the engine, the starter draws much more current than it should.

I have a 1969 Cadillac Fleetwood Sedan. I have a problem getting the starter to turn the engine when the engine is hot. The problem referred to does not occur after brief trips or when the engine is cold. Any suggestion will be appreciated.

In a column about two months ago, I offered several possible solutions to a similar problem. The following letter presents yet another possibility:

"We had a 1964 Bonneville 389 four-barrel that developed a (heating) problem after a ring job.... I had the starter in and out of the car at least 10 times. I could do it from a standing start in less than 10 minutes in my garage, including jacking up the car. No matter what I did, the engine would not crank when it was hot. Finally, through the suggestion of a battery company, I installed the highest amperage battery that would fit in the car. I never had a problem after that."

We have a problem with our 1972 Colt station wagon that is driving us crazy. We have seen similar problems described in your column but none exactly like ours. In hot weather after we've driven 10 or 15 miles and when the motor is shut off for about 10 to 15 minutes, the motor will not restart.

The lights work, the radio will play, but when you turn the key in the ignition, nothing happens. We open the hood for 20 minutes to a half hour and then it starts quickly. We've checked the battery, the solenoid switch, and the starter—and our dealer has gone over the car and can find nothing wrong. Can you offer any suggestions?

As I've said previously, the usual case of problems like this is an underpowered battery due either to age or the fact that the battery is not powerful enough for the use it is put to. Because your car is a subcompact, I doubt the latter. However, since the car is four years old and you say you have checked the battery—not replaced it—your problem might very well be there. I presume when you had it checked, the procedure was with a hydrometer to discern the amount of charge. You might have done it electronically (Fig. 6-1) to check the amount of cranking power since a hot engine demands considerably more than a cold one. There are two other possibilities. One is engine timing. If it's off to any degree, it will make the car hot.

Regarding the letter about the hard-starting car: This happened to me a while back and the problem was diagnosed as a hot starter. That means that when some starters get very warm, the heat increases the electrical resistance and therefore reduces the power output. Sometimes this can be corrected by installing a baffle to keep as much heat as possible away from the starter.

Thanks for the tip.

I recently bought a 24-month battery on sale. I have no complaints about the way it works. It has always started my car with

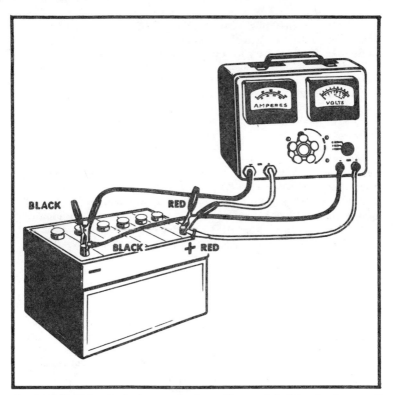

Fig. 6-1. This high-rate discharge procedure will accurately determine the overall condition of a car battery. (Courtesy Chrysler Corp.)

no trouble and even worked the other morning after the parking lights had been left on all night. My question is about the fluid level. I have to add water about once a week. Is this normal?

In a word, no. It is not normal. It would seem there is a problem with your electrical system. It probably is overcharging the battery and boiling away the acid-water mixture. You should have the system analyzed, starting with the voltage regulator.

When I went to start my Volkswagen outside a store, nothing happened. When I turned the key on, even the dashboard warning lights failed to operate. The car was push-started, but as I pulled into my driveway, it failed again. The next morning it started, but the same thing happened again. The battery is four or five years old.

The chances are very good that the cause of your problem is loose battery cables, probably at the battery. The cables should be removed, cleaned, and put back tightly on the same terminals.

Should such a thing happen again when you are away from home, the chances are very good that you can get the car to start by tapping on the battery terminals lightly with a lug wrench. But be careful not to hit it too hard or you might permanently damage the battery.

I have recently purchased a 1976 Chevelle Malibu Classic, Everything is fine except for constant static or interference I get on the FM stereo radio when the engine is running. I took it back to the dealer twice and he claims there is nothing he can do about it since the interference is caused by the electronic ignition system. This is difficult for me to believe. Can this condition be cured?

The condition can be cured fairly simply, and I am a little surprised that your dealer is unaware of how. A Chevrolet engineer says the division has sent out a service bulletin to all dealers informing them of the need to install specific ground straps and static suppressor devices to eliminate these noises. Check with your dealer once more, and if you get no satisfaction, call your local zone office. The number is in the telephone book.

My car's left turn signal recently stopped working—the indicator light on the dashboard just stays on all the time. I bought a new flasher unit and plugged it in under the dashboard, but it still doesn't work. The right turn signal, however, continues to operate. Any ideas?

This is a common misconception. The flasher unit probably is replaced unnecessarily more than any other item on automobiles. The problem in 99 percent of such cases is simply a burned-out bulb at either the front or the rear. Despite the clicking noise you hear when the flasher is operating normally, it is not a mechanical device. Rather, it works in the manner of an electric relay. Depending on the amount of electricity flowing through the system, a switch is opened and closed, making the turn signal flash. That electricity is reduced by 50 percent when one of the bulbs burns out and there isn't enough of a flow to operate the switch. Thus, the one light that still is operating will stay on as will the indicator light on the dashboard. The bulbs—usually dual filament—are easy to replace on most cars. If it is a rear light, the socket probably can be reached from inside the trunk. On the front, it requires the removal of the lens (two or more screws) to gain access to the bulb.

Would you settle a small dispute? A friend and I disagree about whether a car uses any more gasoline when the lights are turned on while the engine is running.

Depending on the number of people you talk to, that's how many valid opinions you'll get on the subject. The theory is that anything that uses power uses energy, in this case supplied by the gasoline. Therefore, the use of headlights will increase gasoline consumption although that increase will be so slight as to be virtually impossible to detect. The other side of the argument is that the same minimal amount of engine power is used to turn the alternator whether accessories are on or not. And it is rare that all the electrical energy produced by the alternator gets through the voltage regulator to the battery for storage. This means that under most conditions, there is some bleed-off or waste of electricity.

My 1973 Ford failed to start. A service center diagnosed alternator failure and installed a new one. The next day the car would not start and the battery had to be changed. I then realized that the time the alternator supposedly was not working, the alternator warning light had not come on. (The light does work with the engine off.)

I presumed that replacing the alternator was an error, but when I confronted the mechanic at the service center, he claimed that an alternator may be run down enough to require replacement yet provide enough charge to keep the warning light off. I find this hard to believe. What do you think?

He is right. A failing alternator can put out enough electricity to keep the warning light off but not enough to operate the car let alone charge the battery (Fig. 6-2). However, this is relatively rare and, unfortunately, a lot of mechanics who operate on the hit-and-miss philosophy use it as an excuse.

The only way to assure yourself of a fair deal in such a situation is to take your car to one of the ever-increasing number of shops that offer—in advance, in writing—to give you the parts that they replace. Had this been the case in your situation, you could have satisfied yourself by having the old alternator bench-tested.

I have a 1968 Mercury Montclair that gives me problems after dark. The lights blink off and on and, eventually, won't come back on. I hit the brakes and the lights will come on. Sometimes, I have stopped the car, turned the lights out, and removed the ignition key. When I start it again, sometimes the blinking continues and sometimes I can get home from as far away as 15 miles. Can you give me any idea what to do about correcting this?

Obviously, the first thing to do is not drive the car at night until you have the problem attended to. It is extremely dangerous, not to mention illegal. I would be inclined to think your problem is something as simple as a loose wire anywhere from the light switch on the dash to the headlights themselves.

You should have the car checked by a technician who specializes in automotive electronics. Another problem area which he undoubtedly will

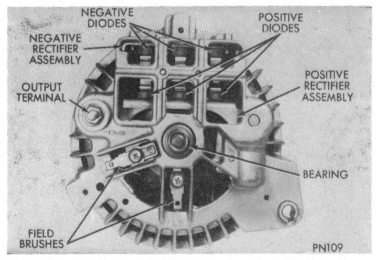

Fig. 6-2. The alternator, heart of a car's electrical system, is comprised of many critical elements, and failure of even one can result in its being ineffective while still operating. (Courtesy Chrysler Corp.)

check is the fuse block. I doubt if there are any problems with the fuses, per se, but this is an area where loose wiring could be prevalent, causing intermittent operation.

I have a 1954 Customline V-8 Ford with a 6-volt electrical system that I would like to convert to 12 volts. I have no real problems with the car except the battery runs down in the winter.

I would not recommend the changeover for several reasons. Foremost is the necessity of going through the entire car and replacing every 6-volt device with 12. That includes every light—from headlamps to the little bulbs that illuminate the dashboard. Then there are the accessories such as the radio and heater blower that must be wired through a voltage step-down device at a loss of efficiency.

The biggest problem would be in the starter and generator. What you would have to do is find a later model with a 12-volt system that has a starter and generator of identical proportions so that they can be bolted to your existing mounting brackets. Incidentally, a 12-volt battery will make a 6-volt starter crank like crazy, but it will not last very long.

Rather than go through all this, I would suggest that you purchase the best quality 6-volt battery you can find. It should give enough cranking power to alleviate your problem.

While driving, I started to hear a sound from the engine compartment like a siren only not quite as loud. I took it to a repair shop where a number of mechanics are employed, a place that does tremendous business.

One of the mechanics put a long metal tube on the motor and said the problem was with the alternator. He replaced the alternator and then put on a new fan belt.

Now I'm wondering if the alternator really was bad or if it just needed a fan belt and I was taken over.

First off, I can only assume that the problem has been corrected—you no longer are getting the noise.

If that's the case, I am relatively certain you got what you paid for. The noise you heard probably was the failing of one of the bearings (almost always the front one) in the alternator. When this happens, it will set up a shrieking noise which rises and falls in direct proportion to how hard you push down on the accelerator.

You can get virtually the same sound when the bearing in the water pump starts to go—hence the rod the mechanic used. It is nothing more than a piece of steel that he places on the housing of the suspected bearing. When a bearing goes, it sets up unusual vibrations which are readily transmitted up the rod to the mechanic's hands. This way he knows immediately where the problem is.

More often than not, this kind of bearing damage is caused by running with the fan belt too tight—there should be about a half inch of play (no more or you'll get slippage which can cause an intermittent shriek and reduce the charge to the battery).

Now you might ask why the mechanic didn't just replace the bearing. It could be done, but it would cost you almost as much money as having a rebuilt one installed.

I own a 1969 Rambler American. The car will not start in cold weather. All I get is a click. The lights and radio continue to work.

The car will start easily by pushing it or using jumper cables. Over the past three years, I have had three new starters installed and two new batteries. Nobody seems able to diagnose the problem. The car is garaged every night. Any ideas?

For your edification, the car you own is a Rambler but it isn't an American. The last Rambler American was built in 1968. For 1969, American Motors built the same car, but dropped the American name.

As to your problem, my first inclination is a problem with either the battery cables or starter relay. If the cables aren't making a good connection at either end, you will get the symptoms you describe. And the jostling about that results from hooking up jumper cables could correct it to the point the car would start.

As for the starter relay, I had a situation develop in which it worked loose from its mounting point on the fender apron and lost its ground. Nothing would happen until the bolts were tightened.

Another possibility is that the battery you have is of the bargain-basement type and it simply doesn't have the power for cold-weather cranking. AMC specifications require a battery with a minimum 50-ampere/hour capacity for your car.

I have a 1967 Chevrolet Caprice. When it was given to me by my father, it hadn't run for about six months and had to be towed to a garage.

They did quite a bit of work on the car, including installing a new battery, for a total cost of $131.92. That was on Nov. 5, 1976. Since that time, the car has failed to start so many times that it has been back seven times at an additional total cost of $181.55. It still isn't right.

The car has a 396-cubic-inch engine, and the mechanic says it just requires a lot of juice to turn the engine over. Now, I am not an expert in car repairs, but they put in a $23.80 battery and that sounds cheap to me. My father says he used to run the car on a battery such as one found in Cadillac. Could this be the problem?

It's obvious from the receipts that you included that the car needed much of the work that was done on it. And on some of the return trips, it appears that unconnected repairs were made.

No matter, the car should not be doing what it is doing. It would seem to me that you have answered your own question. The battery obviously is not up to the job.

The person who told you a 396 Chevy engine requires a lot of juice is correct. That was a tight, high-performance engine and the service manager of the shop should have known that. Of course, it is possible that he didn't have a heavy-duty unit of the proper size for you car and stuck whatever he could in there.

I would go back and insist that they give you full credit for the battery on the cost of the highest ampere-hour battery that will fit your car. If you don't get satisfaction, I would complain to the national headquarters of the company that operates the shop.

The battery in our 1969 Rebel American went dead one zero morning a while ago. The same thing happened after purchasing a new battery, new starter, new solenoid, and new battery cables.

Since then, the car has been to three garages, and each has tested the alternator and voltage regulator under full load, finding them both performing perfectly. All electrical connections have been cleaned and tightened, and the auto electric specialists claim there is no power drain or short circuits anywhere. These towing and garage bills are breaking us up. Can you help?

If it's any consolation, there were thousands of people in the eastern half of the country in the same boat. And the cause of your difficulty probably falls into the one of the same two categories as most everyone else.

The primary culprit in cases like this—where there is absolutely no evidence of power—is a weak battery. The first time it happened, your old battery was simply giving up the ghost.

A lot of people in this situation, thinking they are saving a few bucks, jump on the battery sale bandwagon. They get a battery for, say, $25 with a 24-month guarantee and figure they're in good shape.

Then, the next time the temperature dips sharply, the battery doesn't have the power to do the job because it had less power to start with and the zero weather robs it of more than a third of its charge.

I would check the ampere-hour rating on the side of the battery against the recommended figure in the car's owner's manual. If you have a lower rated battery, the only choice you have is to get one of the recommended size or even larger.

Another possibility is that you have a dead cell in the new battery—they're not necessarily perfect because they're new. If it does have a dead cell, it will drain the charge from the others and this, combined with the subfreezing temperatures, will render it worthless.

Believe it or not, batteries usually are not the primary cause of cars failing to start in the bitter cold. More often than not, the problem is the state of tune of the engine. Most of the time, however, when an engine is in need of a tune-up, a good battery will turn it over awhile. Sometimes however, bad timing can create enough resistance to keep the engine from cranking.

I recently acquired a 1969 Chrysler Imperial with the turn signals inoperative. After searching under the dash for three days for the flasher unit, I finally gave it to a mechanic.

He traced the problem to a small box-like computer in the trunk of the car which he said was part of the turn signals (they flash in sequence). I called several Chrysler-Plymouth dealers, none of whom ever heard of an Imperial with such a device.

I would like to know if that is my flasher unit, and if it can be repaired or replaced by an aftermarket unit (from someone other than Chrysler).

A Chrysler engineer tells me that your mechanic is absolutely correct—the entire flasher unit is contained in the box. What neither he nor I can understand, however, is your not being able to find a mechanic at a Chrysler-Plymouth dealer who understands what you are talking about. Replacement parts up to and including the entire unit are available, although it is doubtful that a dealer would have them in stock.

The best thing you can do is take the car to a dealer, physically show the mechanic what your problem is, and let him take it from there. He will be able to order the part (or parts) needed and will call you when they come in.

Chapter 7
Pollution Control Devices

I bought a 1976 Volare six-cylinder station wagon last February. Immediately afterward, it would not pass the New Jersey emission test. A dealer retarded the spark so it would pass the test but the car would barely run afterwards. I had to take the car back immediately afterward so the dealer could advance the spark and retune the carburetor so the car would function properly on the roar.

But it still isn't right. In cold weather the car keeps stalling, and the motor goes dead when I step on the gas until the car has been driven at least five miles or more.

Can you offer any suggestions or explanations?

The problem of meeting emission control regulations under varying climatic conditions is difficult, if not impossible. There are so many variables that it would be impossible to single out any one as the cause of your problem.

And it isn't limited to six-cylinder Chrysler products, either. It seems that in the laboratory-controlled tests that the Environmental Protection Agency uses, conditions are optimum for reasonable operation of engines. On top of this, the manufacturers are allowed to have technicians on hand to make minor adjustments throughout the 50,000-mile tests.

In actual practice, as you and millions of others have discovered to their dismay, things aren't so rosy. Most cars buck and stall and generally run poorly until they are warmed up. You just notice it more in winter because it takes more time.

The EPA is fully cognizant of the problem and has initiated changes in the test that will require the manufacturers to improve the situation, if not cure it all together. Unfortunately, this will not help you.

It may seem like a criminal act, but you'll have to do like most other people do—live up to the letter of the law but not the spirit. You'll have to have the car tuned twice a year—once before inspection and once after.

As for the stalling, several possibilities (mostly in carburetion) were discussed in a recent column. And a reader has suggested yet another that sounds logical: deactivate the automatic choke electronic heater unit. This device supplies warm air to the carburetor intake and can, if not working properly, cause the choke to open too soon, resulting in a fuel-air mixture that is not rich enough. It is located along the thermostatic spring on the manifold which controls the choke lever. To deactivate, simply pull off one of the wires and tape it back. Since this unit is controlled by a timed relay, it is possible that replacing the relay might solve the problem.

I have a 1976 Chrysler Cordoba with 4,500 miles on it. Can you tell me what causes that horrible rotten egg smell which emits from my car when it is idling or when I'm parking in my garage? Also, will it burn off as the dealer advises?

The rancid odor is caused by sulfur oxide, which is a byproduct of the chemical process by which the harmful pollutants in a car's exhaust are rendered much less harmful.

What happens is that in most 1975 and 1976 model cars, the exhaust gases are forced through a device known as a catalytic converter which, when operating at a very high temperature, in effect burns off the carbon monoxide and unburned hydrocarbons. The result is a sulfur oxide which most experts say is harmless although it is believed to be a problem in sufficient quantities. At any rate, virtually all cars sold in the United States since the start of the 1975 model year emit this substance.

Some, however, give off a much stronger odor than others—there seems to be no way of knowing in advance whether it will or not. Some, as your dealer says, will give off less odor as time progresses. Others however, have been known to get worse.

By the way, your car is giving off the same amount of odor at all times. It's just not as noticeable when you're driving because the wind carries it behind you (to offend the nostrils of following motorists).

I own a 1975 Buick Century with a 231-cubic-inch V-6 engine. My problem has been hesitation on acceleration. I solved this by removing the EGR (exhaust gas recirculation) valve hose. I got smooth acceleration except that the engine started to ping a lot. I eliminated that by retarding the timing.

Do you think what I did will do any damage to the engine? I would like to know before I cause any permanent problems.

The only permanent damage you will cause is to the blood pressure of the folks at the Environmental Protection Agency. You see, what you have done is to effectivley bypass a part of the emission control system—and EPA doesn't like that.

As a matter of fact, you are leaving yourself open for a whole lot of trouble because tampering with automotive emission control systems is against the law and is punishable by fine, imprisonment, or both.

Now to your original problem—hesitation. I have tested several cars equipped with the Buick V-6 and, more often than not, have experienced the same thing. In all but one of the cases, it went away as soon as the engine reached operating temperatures. In the other instance, it was corrected by adjusting the fast idle.

My advice is to put things back the way they were and take them to a competent technician who has sufficient diagnostic equipment to eliminate the hesitation.

Why does a car make a popping sound? This happens when I am driving and my car seems to slow and nearly stop. The sound seems to be coming from under the rear of the car, a six-cylinder Chevrolet Nova. Any advice will be appreciated.

There are at least two possible causes, one being backfiring and the other a malfunction of the antipollution pop-off valve.

If the problem is backfiring, this can be due to improper timing (Fig. 7-1) or a bad exhaust valve. The usual cause is bad ignition timing, which is not difficult or expensive to have repaired. The timing is what controls the firing of the spark plugs in relation to the other parts of the engine. If the timing is excessively retarded, the engine will backfire through the exhaust system because the explosion occurs while the exhaust valve is open.

If it's a bad exhaust valve, the combustion chamber explosion will create a backfire no matter what the timing is set at. Should this be the case, it will entail a valve job, which could cost you more than $100 since it is a major repair.

Either way, you should have it attended to as soon as possible to prevent further damage, not to mention the possibility of the engine shutting off completely at some inopportune moment.

I would like to know if the new cars would run better without the catalytic converter and other pollution stuff on them. Is regular gas better for the car than unleaded gas?

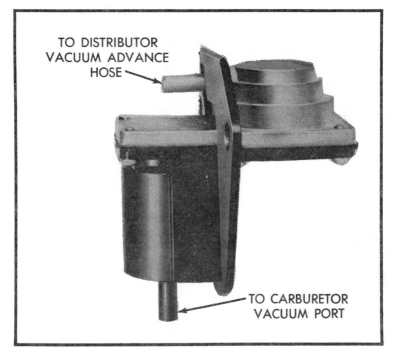

TO DISTRIBUTOR VACUUM ADVANCE HOSE

TO CARBURETOR VACUUM PORT

Fig. 7-1. Among the pollution control gadgets that can foul ignition timing if they're not operating properly is Orifice Spark Advance Control (Courtesy Chrysler Corp.)

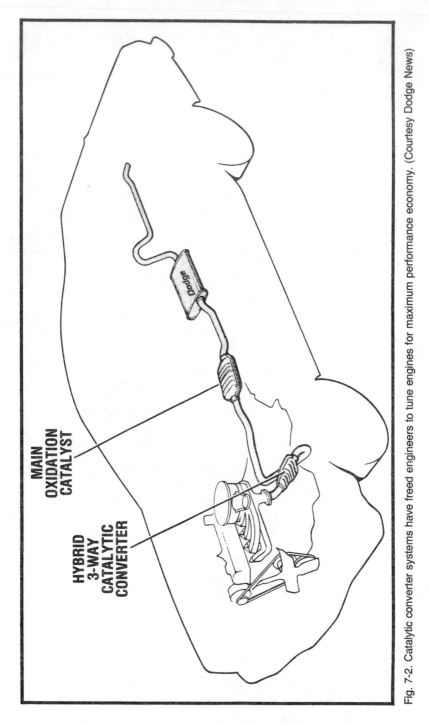

MAIN
OXIDATION
CATALYST

HYBRID
3-WAY
CATALYTIC
CONVERTER

Fig. 7-2. Catalytic converter systems have freed engineers to tune engines for maximum performance economy. (Courtesy Dodge News)

You probably wouldn't notice much difference if the catalytic converter and other devices on recent models were removed. The converter (Fig. 7-2) in fact, has made it possible for the engineers to more efficiently tune car engines. Prior to the introduction of catalysts (1974 and earlier models), emissions were controlled by such "detuning" practices as retarding the spark to make the engine run hotter and burn off the pollutants. This reduced both fuel mileage and performance, while increasing wear and tear.

As for regular gas versus unleaded, the best solution is to use exactly the type fuel the manufacturer stipulates. In other words, cars that were designed to run on leaded (either regular or premium) gas will perform better when it is used. As for cars designed to use unleaded fuel, the introduction of lead would, in a very brief time, burn out the catalytic converter and greatly increase the pollutants.

We have a 1975 six-cylinder Valiant. After we drive it a couple of blocks and stop, then start again, the car stops as if it gets no gas. What do you suggest?

Ever since we got serious about fighting pollution in general and automobile emissions in particular, the state of a car's tune has become increasingly critical. There are numerous variables that must be taken into consideration, some of which can cause any number of problems if they aren't exactly on the mark.

Your complaint is one that I frequently get, especially from owners of Chrysler products. Most people say the cars run perfectly at all times except when they are cold.

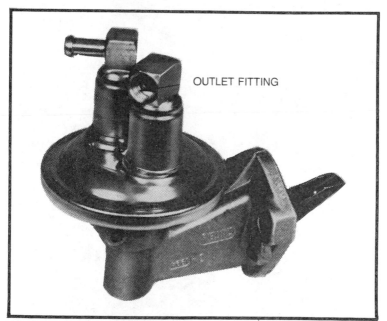

OUTLET FITTING

Fig. 7-3. Less than normal fuel pump pressure can cause stalling problems. A cursory check can be made in minutes by holding your finger over the large-diameter outlet fitting and cranking the engine. (Courtesy Chrysler Corp.)

61

AUTOMATIC
CHOKE CONTROL
ASSEMBLY

Fig. 7-4. The automatic choke can cause problems, but more often than not the trouble is elsewhere. (Courtesy AMC)

There are three areas that could cause your problem, two of which involve the fuel system. The usual culprit in cases like this is the carburetor whose exact calibration is crucial. Likely carburetor problems include an accelerator pump that is dirty or inoperative due to mechanical problems such as bent linkage. The accelerator pump jets also might not be directed properly. And, if the float level is too low, the engine most certainly will starve for fuel.

Another area to check is the fuel pump (Fig. 7-3). If it isn't putting out the proper volume and pressure, hesitation will always come into play. The pump should deliver at least a pint of fuel every 40 seconds.

Lastly is the ignition timing. If it is off the mark just a whisker, it will cause your symptoms, and they generally will persist even after the engine is warmed up.

When starting my 1974 truck (10,000 miles), it kicks right off. But as soon as I go about 20 feet, it quits and does the same thing four or five times before it finally gets going. It only seems to happen when the engine is cold. Mechanics tell me everything is okay, but I think there's something wrong with the automatic choke.

Although there *could* be a problem with the automatic choke (Fig. 7-4), it most likely is a sign of the times. Assuming your truck is a pickup or a van or something else in the "light " category, it is subjected to virtually the same emission regulations as passenger cars (bigger trucks are exempted from most of those rules). The problem is that to meet emission standards in that pre-catalytic converter year, engines were detuned to run hotter (and much less efficiently) so as to burn off as much of the pollutants as possible. There are other factors that contribute to the overall inefficiency of engines of this vintage, but to keep them running at anything near acceptable levels, they must be maintained at or near the manufacturer's tuning specifications. This also will keep your gas mileage at its best.

When I start my 1974 six-cylinder Dodge Dart S.E., I have to keep the accelerator to the floor before it will start—even when it's warmed up.

As I slow up to make a left turn and start to accelerate in the turn, it dies. Absolutely nothing.

Don't say it's just me because it does the same thing for my son.

You may have one of a few problems all related to the flow of fuel to your engine, but your biggest trouble is something that afflicts most cars of 1974 vintage—pollution controls. Hard starting is one of the effects of the detuning process used before 1975 to reduce exhaust emissions.

Other things that would aggravate the situation—and especially cause stalling in turns—are those that would impede the flow of fuel, such as dirt or water in the fuel and improper jets in the carburetor. There also could be trouble with the automatic choke (Fig. 7-4).

A simple check by a service facility with complete diagnostic equipment should be able to determine the trouble quickly.

Chapter 8
Cooling Systems

I have a 1973 Vega GT with a radiator problem. The car is equipped with a coolant recovery tank to keep the radiator full. However coolant no longer flows to the recovery tank when hot and no longer flows to the radiator when cool, despite replacing the radiator cap and tubing to the recovery tank.

After filling the cold radiator and then running the car, a later check of the coolant level shows a decrease. But the coolant recovery tank remains unchanged. Checks of the oil show no water contamination. My local dealer has pressure-tested the radiator and it checks out okay. He's stumped. I'm stumped. Any ideas?

Obviously, the coolant is somehow escaping to the outside. You seem to have eliminated the most obvious possibilities—assuming you have the new coolant recovery hose properly attached to the radiator's overflow pipe (Fig. 8-1).

One other possibility might be a crack or small hole in the recovery tank that would allow fluid to leave the system there. It also would eliminate the vacuum upon which the system works.

Another possibility is a seep crack somewhere in the block that permits coolant to seep to the outside under the pressure of heating up. This could also happen with a bad freeze plug that would allow leakage. Along the same lines, a failing head gasket could permit a slow leak.

Last, it is possible that trapped air somewhere in the cooling system doesn't allow you to completely fill with coolant. This can make the engine run hotter than normal and could cause your symptoms, although fluid loss would be minimal.

I was driving my new Plymouth Valiant (1,000 miles on it) along the Pennsylvania Turnpike recently when I noticed that the temperature gauge indicated more than 250 degrees. I stopped

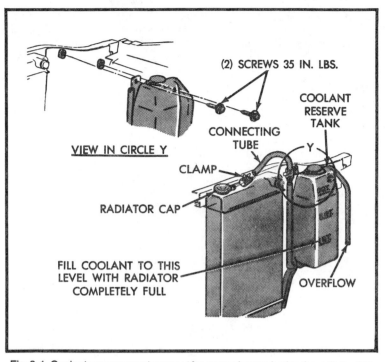

(2) SCREWS 35 IN. LBS.

COOLANT
RESERVE
TANK

CONNECTING
TUBE

VIEW IN CIRCLE Y

CLAMP

RADIATOR CAP

FILL COOLANT TO THIS
LEVEL WITH RADIATOR
COMPLETELY FULL

OVERFLOW

Fig. 8-1. Coolant recovery system must be properly attached to the radiator if it is to function correctly. (Courtesy Chrysler Corp.)

the car, turned the engine off, and lifted the hood. I found that the fan belt was broken, and the coolant was boiling.

About 20 minutes later, a passing motorist told me there was a service area about two miles away and I could drive there without the fan at a speed of no more than 30 miles per hour.

When I got there, the temperature was still above 250 degrees and the coolant continued to boil. The belt was replaced and the lost coolant replaced. I continued my trip and have had no problem since.

I would like to know what damage could have occurred to the engine under those conditions.

Depending on how far you drove the car before noticing that the temperature was very high, damage could range from nothing to extensive. But because you notice no real problems, I would say that damage is miniscule, if it exists at all.

As a precaution, however, I would have the engine oil (and filter) changed as early as convenient. This is because as the temperature of the oil increases, so do the chances of its breaking down and, thereby, losing some of its lubricating qualities.

I also would check the condition of the transmission fluid because it might have suffered damage since the transmission oil cooler is an integral part of the radiator.

If there are traces of brown or black in the normally bright red transmission fluid, have it changed, too. This discoloration would indicate a "burning" of the fluid, which could lead to expensive problems.

I drive a 1972 Oldsmobile 98 with 70,000 miles on it and have no major problems. However, on a few trips over the last few years—always in hot weather and usually with the air conditioning on— I have experienced what can best be described as a vapor cloud coming out of the engine compartment. On one occasion it made a noise similar to that of an engine running hot. There never have been any indications of trouble through gauges or warning lights, and the car never has failed to run. I never have had any problem with excessive oil consumption, although the right side valve cover does show a slight leak. Any ideas?

The noise you heard like an overheating engine probably was exactly that. In hot weather with the air conditioner running full tilt, the cooling system of any vehicle will be put to a severe test. What probably is happening to you is that the temperature buildup increases the pressure inside your car's cooling system to the point that the pressure release spring in your radiator cap opens to allow some of the steam to escape—thus the vapor cloud you are seeing.

It is not exactly normal but nothing to get overly worried about unless repeated occurrences deplete the amount of coolant to a degree that the engine could be damaged. I would check the radiator cap carefully to make sure it is of the right pressure rating and in good condition. If you have any doubts replace it. I also would check the radiator warning light system. If things get hot enough to pop the pressure spring, the light should go on.

Most of all, keep a constant check on the level of coolant in the radiator—but be sure to do this only when the engine is cool. There are two reasons for that. First, even under normal operating conditions, the expansion would give you an inaccurate reading; second, when it's hot it'll come out like a geyser and can severely burn you.

I recently obtained a low-mileage 1966 Ford with a 390 V-8 engine. I had no problems until the first warm day when the temperature shot up. It has never boiled over but always seems to run hot even though I removed the thermostat. Any ideas?

Believe it or not, an engine will run hotter in warm weather with no thermostat than with one (Fig. 8-2). Assuming you removed the stock 190-degree thermostat, I would recommend installing a 160-degree unit. You should notice an improvement.

I have a 1967 Dodge Polara sedan with a little over 37,000 miles on the odometer. I may add that my car looks like it just came off the sales floor, as I take care of it inside and out. I recently had the valve cover gaskets replaced to correct an oil leak, and my mechanic advised me that, since my radiator is full of rust, I should have a reverse or back flush done to the cooling system. I heard some years ago that this can cause a whole host of problems, including leaks. Can you advise on the feasibility of a reverse flush?

I have never heard of a reverse flush causing leaks that weren't already there. It is possible that the core of your radiator has deteriorated to such a

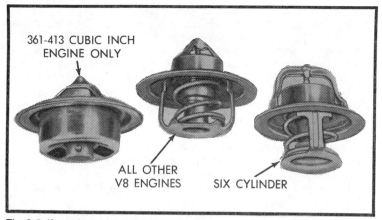

361-413 CUBIC INCH
ENGINE ONLY

ALL OTHER
V8 ENGINES   SIX CYLINDER

Fig. 8-2. If you do not have the proper thermostat for given conditions, the car's engine may not operate at the proper temperature. (Courtesy Chrysler Corp.)

degree from the buildup of rust and corrosion that several areas are weak enough to leak soon. If this is the case, all the reverse flush might do is hasten the process. In the overwhelming majority of cases, however, a reverse flush can do nothing but improve the condition of your system. If you don't have it done, the radiator will continue to deteriorate to a point where you'll have a very expensive repair bill on your hands.

I have a 1964 Ford station wagon. My problem is that every morning I have to add a half a teakettle of water to the radiator. I checked the oil and it is creamy. I also had a compression check and all the cylinders run between 85 and 100 pounds, except one which was 50. Any suggestions?

If you had the compression check done by a mechanic, he probably told you the same thing I am going to tell you. The problem most likely is a blown head gasket.

The gasket has failed between journals that carry water and oil to the cylinder head from the block and from the compression chamber of the 50-pound cylinder to either or both of those journals. What is happening is that water is seeping into the oil, causing it to foam and turn creamy.

The biggest problem created by operating an engine in this condition is that the water quickly contaminates the oil and greatly reduces its lubricating properties.

If the overall condition of the car warrants the investment of $50 – $100, I would have the gasket replaced as soon as possible.

I have a 1968 Buick Skylark with a V-8 engine. I have had a new thermostat and water pump installed and the radiator dismantled and cleaned. However, apparently I'm still losing water and no one seems to be able to correct the problem. Can you offer any suggestions?

If fluid loss isn't visible externally, there is only one way it can be going through the inside of the engine. And that, I'm sorry to say, usually indicates a blown head gasket. There are two ways you can lose coolant internally. One is if the gasket fails between a water and oil journal. Should this be the case, you would notice a gradual increase in the level of the oil. Also, if you check the dipstick immediately after running the engine, water-polluted oil would show up as a milky gray color. The other possibility is if the gasket failed between a water journal and the combustion chamber. In this case, the coolant would seep into the chamber and be burned with the fuel-air mixture. Condensation, however, would show up in the tailpipe.

I have a 1969 Dodge Charger 318. In the hot months my cooling system gets very hot when I stop and go in traffic. Let the car just idle and the system is okay.

I have flushed out the system, changed thermostats, had the radiator cored, made sure the timing was right, and done every possible thing the repair manual specifies. In the winter, the cooling system is okay.

If you can come up with any kind of answer, I would appreciate it.

It sounds as though you might have some obstruction to the flow of air to and/or through your radiator. Make sure the entire grill area is clear of debris, and try using an air hose on the back of the radiator to force out any bugs, bits of paper, or leaves that might have collected.

While you're in that area, make sure you have enough tension on your fan belt (Fig. 8-3). If it is loose, the engine can speed up, especially in stop and go traffic, without a corresponding increase in fan speed.

As a last resort, I would try running pure ethylene glycol in the cooling system with no thermostat at all. If this works, you should reinstall the thermostat each fall (or you won't get much heat from your heater), but that's a small price to pay.

My car is a 1972 Dodge, six-cylinder Coronet, and there is a noise that sounds like metal against metal around the fan assembly and water pump. What is the problem and what would be the approximate repair bill?

The chances are very good that there is a bad bearing in either the water pump or the alternator (which is driven off the same belt system). If it is the former, which is more likely the case, the repair bill should be less than $35, assuming your shop will install a rebuilt pump rather than a new one. If it is the latter, a rebuilt alternator and installation could go as high as $50.

A good test to determine where the problem lies is to take a long steel rod and place it against the suspected part. The grinding that you hear sets up vibrations that are easily transmitted through the rod to your hand.

There is a remote possibility that your problem is minor—a loose fan belt. When this is the case, the engine will make a shrieking (rather than a grinding) noise when the accelerator pedal is blipped, but will be quiet under most other conditions. If this is the case, a simple adjustment will solve the problem.

What could cause three water pumps to fail in two years and 9,000 miles? The last one went so violently that it damaged the radiator and resulted in a huge bill.

The service people deny any responsibility. However I am wondering if the pumps could have been defective or even used rather than new. Could it be faulty installation?

If all this has taken place in 9,000 miles since the car was purchased new, there could be a defect on the mounting surface of the block that doesn't allow the pump to seat properly. Then the shaft and pulley would always be at an improper angle and under severe strain at all times. If that is the case, you have a legitimate claim against the automaker.

I doubt very much if the shop is installing used water pumps, but they may be using cut-rate rebuilt parts that, obviously, aren't as good as new or certified remanufactured pieces.

There also could be a weight imbalance in the fan blades which are not replaced along with the pump unit. With the fan turning several times a minute, this imbalance would unduly strain the shaft and bearing.

Lastly, it's possible that the fan belt is adjusted too tightly causing excess strain. You could check that yourself by moving the belt (or belts) up and down. There should be about a half inch of play.

I have an 1977 Olds Cutlass 260 V-8. Connected to the radiator is a see-through container indicating the water/

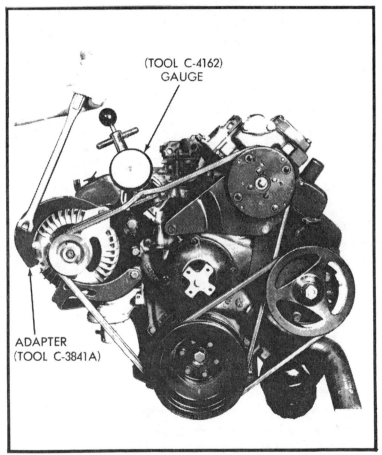

Fig. 8-3. There are special tools to make sure fan belt tension is right, but in a pinch you can get that half inch of play just by using a prybar and a wrench. (Chrysler Corp. Photo)

antifreeze level. **During a recent weekend trip at highway speeds I heard a gurgling sound coming from that see-through tank.** The **anti-freeze expanded in the container and was "bubbling," yet no overheating red light showed on the dash indicator. Can you tell me what the problem is, if any?**

I don't think you have any problem—unless you notice a significant drop in the fluid level, which you didn't mention. Most likely, the gurgling and bubbling you hear is the air being forced from the cooling system by the normal expansion of the coolant as it gets hot. This expansion also would account for the fluid level rising in the catch tank.

I have a perplexing problem with a 1975 Toyota Celica. The car will not reach operating temperature in cold weather. I have replaced the thermostat, checked the gauge, and made sure that the system does not leak. Right now I am running with a piece of cardboard blocking on most of the radiator, but I don't see that this is safe to do. What could be the problem?

Most likely, the trouble is that you installed the wrong degree thermostat. For virtually all water-cooled cars there are three thermostats available for various operating conditions. The average breakdown is at 160 degrees, 180, and 200.

If, as I suspect, you are operating with a 160-degree thermostat, the car will never warm up completely in cold weather conditions.

As for blocking the radiator with a piece of cardboard, that's a trick that's been used for years to achieve the same effect. If temperature conditions remain constantly cold, it will get the job done for you without undue risk. However, if there is a fluctuation in temperature, bitter cold one day and warm the next, you do run the risk of overheating.

Back to the thermostat for a minute. If you want to check the one you have, you can do it simply in your kitchen. With a thermometer that goes up to 212 degrees Fahrenheit, put a pot of water on the stove. When it gets to about 150, drop the thermostat in the water. Keep an eye on the thermostat and when it opens, just check the temperature.

I have a 1974 Dodge Sportsman van equipped with a 318 engine, power steering, power brakes, and air conditioning. On extremely hot days, the engine operates uncomfortably hot— about 200 to 208 degrees—especially when stopping in traffic, which is understandable.

This summer, we plan a rather long trip during our vacation. We will be hauling an extra 800 to 1,000 pounds—motorcycle and camping gear. I have always taken good care of the cooling system and keep a good coolant in all year. Should I expect any problems and, if so, what would you recommend?

First off, since your van was built in the last year that the manufacturers controlled emissions by means of the "plumber's nightmare" that included retardation of the ignition, it is natural that it will run hotter than might be desired.

However, you probably have a thermostat of at least 190 − 200 degrees, and you might get some relief by switching to a 160-degree unit.

As for the trip, I don't think you will run into any particular problem with up to 1,000 pounds. Last year, I hauled a camper trailer with supplies for a

70

family of five several thousand miles without the slightest sign of overheating on a 1976 Dodge Maxiwagon.

However, if you are going to do a lot of driving in especially hot areas such as the southwest or plan to put additional strain on the vehicle by driving up and down mountains, you might be advised to add transmission oil cooler.

There are several add-on units available. One of the best is a simple bolt-on cooler offered by Hurst Performance of Warminster, Pa. It bolts immediately in front of the radiator, and the lines running from the transmission to the stock in-radiator cooler are hooked to the separate unit.

Chapter 9
Heaters and Air Conditioners

The service manager where we bought our 1975 Matador told us that our car does not have a water valve and that, therefore, we get hot water through the heater all the time. He advised not opening the right air vent to keep out the heat, which is unbearable down by our feet in summer driving. American Motors phoned us confirming this some time ago and said it had issued a technical bulletin to correct the situation. So far nothing. What do you recommend?

AMC engineers say a few Matadors were built without the shut-off valves and that your service manager should be aware of the issuance of Technical Bulletin #3, Group 13, dated Jan. 28, 1975. If he isn't, tell him to call the AMC Tech Line in Detroit for information.

The problem of heat always emanating from a car's heater can be solved very simply by having an on-off petcock installed at an easily accessible spot on one of the heater hoses under the car's hood (Fig. 9-1). In summer, the flow can be cut off and for winter it can very simply be turned back on.

I have a 1973 Oldsmobile Delta 88 and am unable to get sufficient heat from the heater to keep the car even reasonably warm. This problem existed even when the car was new, and the dealer supposedly tried everything to rectify the situation but to no avail. Any suggestions?

I can think of two primary possibilities, either of which should have been discovered by a mechanic who "supposedly tried everything."

The most likely culprit is the wrong thermostat. If you have a 160-degree thermostat, the water from the radiator will start circulating when engine coolant temperature reaches 160 degrees. Although that may seem hot to you, it is cold by engine operating standards. Make sure that there is a 190- or 200-degree thermostat that will keep the temperature up.

Secondly, if your radiator's coolant level is down by a couple of quarts, it may be enough to bypass the heater system, resulting in mostly cold air.

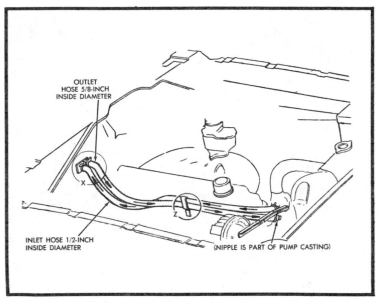

OUTLET
HOSE 5/8-INCH
INSIDE DIAMETER

X

Z

?

INLET HOSE 1/2-INCH
INSIDE DIAMETER

(NIPPLE IS PART OF PUMP CASTING)

Fig. 9-1. The installation of a simple on-off petcock in one of the heater hoses provides easy elimination of summer heat buildup. (Courtesy Chrysler Corp.)

A remote possibility is that the lever that controls your temperature isn't opening and closing valves as it should. No matter what, if you block off part of the radiator with a piece of cardboard, it'll make it run hotter. But be careful not to overheat if you try this.

We own a 1974 Volkswagen Thing, which we bought second hand. We have had continual trouble with the gas heater on this car—every month it breaks down, which has proven inconvenient as well as chilly. I've heard a rumor that VW is giving rebates on the Thing because of faulty gas heaters.

Your problem leaves me at something of a loss because, from all I've seen and heard, the VW gasoline heaters are both dependable and efficient. However, there is a distinct possibility that you dealer is not familiar enough with them to effect a permanent repair. You might try another dealer or write to VW of America, Englewood Cliffs, N.J., for help. Incidentally, there are no rebates or guarantees beyond the 12-month, 12,000-mile warranty.

When I turn on my car's defroster, the condensation on the windshield seems to get worse instead of clearing away. Can you explain?

It sounds like you have developed a slight leak in your car's heater coil. When you turn on your defroster, the resultant liquid is turned to steam by the heat and blown up the defroster ducts to the windshield where it aggravates the situation.

Depending on the year and model of your car and the accessories (specifically air conditioning), it can be a very complicated job. The heater must be dismantled and the coil disconnected and removed (Fig. 9-2).

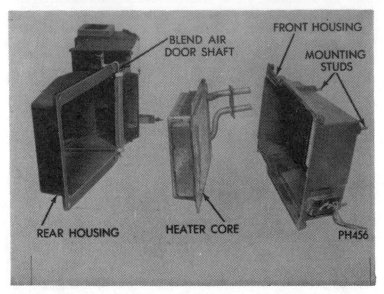

BLEND AIR
DOOR SHAFT

FRONT HOUSING

MOUNTING
STUDS

REAR HOUSING   HEATER CORE   PH456

Fig. 9-2. To remove the heater coil, dismantle the ductwork on the firewall at the right side under the dash and pull the coil free. Hoses from the heater may be fastened on either side of the firewall and must be disconnected. (Courtesy Chrysler Corp.)

Unlike the standard car radiator, a heater coil should not be repaired. It must be replaced because it is under much greater pressure and most likely would soon develop another leak if you should try to have it soldered.

I have a 1972 Mercury Montego with 25,000 miles on it. I am having a constant problem with the air conditioning system, which was never good from the time the car was new. Several months ago it gave up completely, putting out nothing but hot air.

I had the system completely overhauled—new compressor and expansion valve and about five cans of freon. It works good to fair when the car is first started after sitting all night. But after the engine warms up, the air is no longer even cool. Do you have any suggestions?

The first thing I would check is the condition and tension of the compressor drive belt in any situation involving automotive air conditioning problems. This is one of the most common causes of insufficient cooling. Unlike your generator/water pump belt, which should be adjusted to about ½ inch of play, there should be no more than ¼ inch of play in the compressor belt. And, should your belt be replaced, you should recheck the tightness.

There are of course, numerous other possibilities. You might be getting enough cooling but insufficient air flow, in which case the blower motor may be failing (Fig. 9-3) or the evaporator coil could be clogged.

If the trouble is in the refrigeration unit itself, it might be caused by moisture, air, or excess refrigerant in the system. A defective thermostat or a partially clogged screen in the expansion valve could also mess up the works.

There are other possibilities too numerous to mention here. I would suggest having it checked by an auto air conditioning specialist.

We are driving a 1976 Ford LTD with approximately 6,000 miles on it. The problem is with the air conditioning system. A musty odor comes out of the system when the lever is moved from air conditioning to economy vent.

When the heat is on, the musty odor also is present, but it usually isn't as bad. The dealer tells us that water or condensation is lying in the system, and he does not know what to do about it.

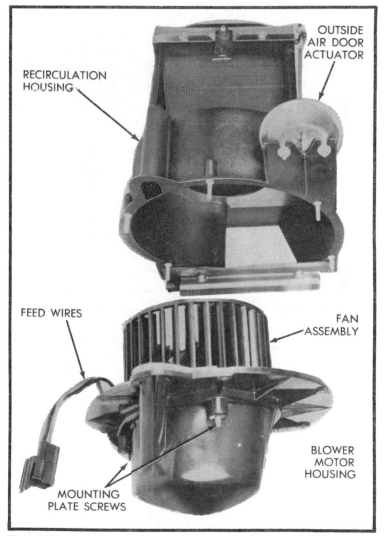

Fig. 9-3. The air conditioning blower motor is serviced from inside the car, on the right-hand side under the dashboard. (Courtesy Chrysler Corp.)

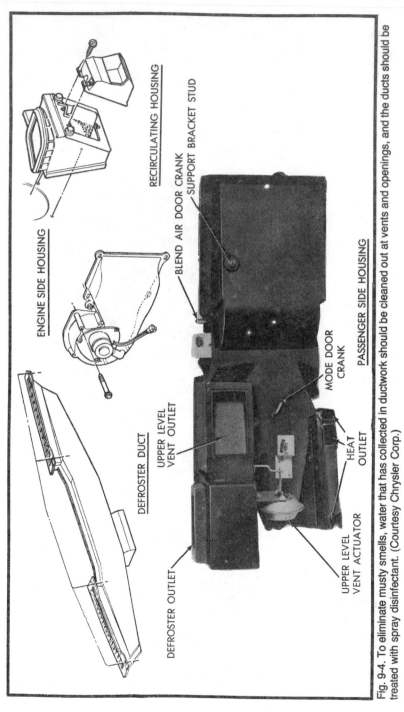

ENGINE SIDE HOUSING

RECIRCULATING HOUSING

DEFROSTER DUCT

UPPER LEVEL VENT OUTLET

BLEND AIR DOOR CRANK SUPPORT BRACKET STUD

MODE DOOR CRANK

PASSENGER SIDE HOUSING

HEAT OUTLET

DEFROSTER OUTLET

UPPER LEVEL VENT ACTUATOR

Fig. 9-4. To eliminate musty smells, water that has collected in ductwork should be cleaned out at vents and openings, and the ducts should be treated with spray disinfectant. (Courtesy Chrysler Corp.)

This musty smell is giving us a headache. What can we do?
There are three probable causes for this situation. As your dealer informed you, the cause is most often water in the system. This water is formed through condensation on the air conditioning evaporator and falls into drains that aren't evacuating properly. The water becomes stagnant and this is the source of the smell.

If you'll look under the dashboard, you'll notice some small doors and vents in ductwork (Fig. 9-4). You can get most of the water out by using a rag, and if you feel around with your finger you should find the faulty drain, which can be cleaned with your finger. Once done, a shot of disinfectant should get rid of the smell very quickly.

Another cause can be your windshield washer solvent. Some of these commercial products smell to high heaven. If used a great deal, the ventilation system can pick up the odor.

The third possibility is that during assembly, the heater coil was shoved too far into position. This can allow the ethylene glycol anti-freeze coolant mixture to seep into the air conditioning vents, causing a bad smell.

I have a problem with my 1971 Delta 88 Oldsmobile. The blower fan motor has gotten noisy in the last six months and is getting worse. Can you tell me where it is located and how to get at it? My shop manual is no help.
You didn't indicate whether your car is equipped with air conditioning or not. But, since the majority of Deltas are equipped with air, I'll gamble that that's the case. The location is different in cars not so equipped.

You must get at it through the right front wheel well, obviously jacking up the car, securing it with a stand, and removing the wheel. When under the hood, remove the charcoal cannister that's part of the anti-pollution equipment. Then unfasten the bolts which attach the radiator supports to the filler panel. Then remove the bolts that secure the wheel arch and take off the right-hand wheel arch filler panel. That will expose the blower motor. To replace, simply reverse the procedures.

Chapter 10
Transmissions and Running Gear

While driving my MGB the other evening, I heard a shearing noise followed by a sound something like putting a pencil on a fan. At that point, the car seemed to lose power. It remains in gear and is impossible to shift. Is the problem something I could repair myself?

From your description of the symptoms, it sounds very much like you have serious clutch problems. The shearing noise followed by the sound of a pencil being hit by a fan indicates failure of the throw-out bearing.

The loss of power probably isn't really a loss of power. It is slipping of the clutch or the failure of the clutch to transfer engine power to the rest of the drive train. What probably is happening is that as you further depress the accelerator, the engine speed increases much faster than the car itself.

The fact that it is impossible to shift is further indication of trouble in this area in that it is impossible to disengage the clutch even when the pedal is fully depressed.

This is a major job: the driveshaft must be disconnected and the transmission removed to permit access to the clutch assembly.

All clutches consist of three main parts—the disc, pressure plate, and throw-out bearing (Fig. 10-1). The disc is a circular piece of abrasive that physically transmits the engine's power to the transmission.

The pressure plate is a spring-loaded device that activates the disc and is connected to the clutch pedal through the throw-out bearing and several pieces of linkage.

Repairing the problem is a job that will cost somewhere between $150 and $250. All three parts of the clutch assembly should be replaced ($50 to $75), even if one or more appear to have some service left in them. The reason is that most of the cost of the job is labor, and a used piece could necessitate all the work over again.

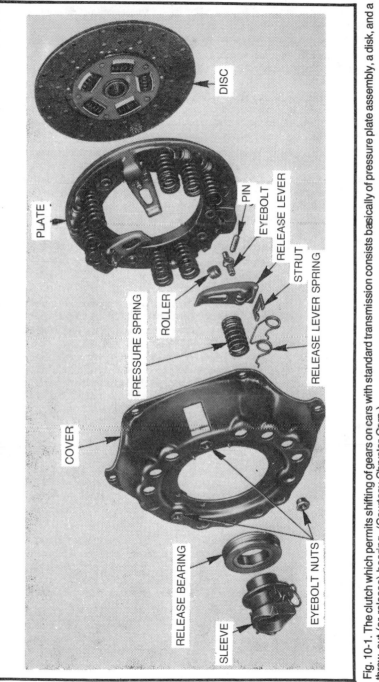

Fig. 10-1. The clutch which permits shifting of gears on cars with standard transmission consists basically of pressure plate assembly, a disk, and a throw-out (or release) bearing. (Courtesy Chrysler Corp.)

79

Although it is possible to drive the car in this condition, it is highly ill-advised. You can't do any more damage to the clutch, but the transmission is in jeopardy and that would cost a lot more to repair.

I am faced with a dilemma: my clutch freezes. Every time the temperature dips below 32 degrees, the clutch pedal of my 1968 VW bus becomes stiff. Most times after warming the engine and 10 minutes of pumping, the clutch returns to normal. However, when it gets down to single-digit temperatures, nothing works. No mechanic or repair manual provides a solution. Please help before spring.

The clutch on your VW is operated by a tube-enclosed cable that runs from the base of the pedal to the activating arm on the side of the trans-axles bell-housing. On occasion, moisture can seep into this tube and, as the temperature drops, it will cause the cable to seize. Then, as you warm the engine and provide further heat through friction as you pump the pedal, the cable frees itself. And, as you say, the colder it gets, the less likely it is that this solution will work.

To cure it, you'll have to disconnect the cable at either end and pull it out of the tube. Then use compressed air to blow any collected moisture out of the tube. To prevent its recurrence, pack the tube lightly with lubricating grease as you feed the cable tack through.

I have a 1976 Nova with a 2.73 axle ratio. I attempted to get a 2.56 axle but it was not available (it was an option in 1975 and was standard in 1977). A mechanic told me he could put a 2.56 gear in the differential for between $80 and $100.

I would like to know what effect this change would have on the car's performance and its economy. Would changing the rear axle affect all gears or just third? Also, would I get better traction on snow and ice if I used FR70-14 snow tires instead of FR78-14s?

I am sure that what you have in mind is to increase the car's fuel economy without decreasing its performance. Unfortunately, there is no way to do this.

The rear axle ratio figure is nothing more than the rate at which the drive shaft turns in comparison to the rotation of the rear axles which drive the wheels. For instance, the setup you now have will require 2.73 turns of the driveshaft for every axle revolution. If you reduce that to 2.56-to-1, you will cut down on the performance. Regardless of the rear axle ratio, the transmission is the same.

If the overwhelming majority of your driving is at constant highway speeds, you could realize a fuel saving of as much as 10 percent. If you drive mostly in stop-and-go situations, you probably won't save any fuel. Either way, acceleration will fall off accordingly.

As to the tires, you might realize slightly more traction because the lower profile of the 70 series tire puts slightly more rubber on the road. However, since 70s usually cost more than 78s, it might not be worth it.

When my 1969 Ford Galaxie has been in use with the engine warmed up, I find that when I slow down to under 30 miles per hour and then accelerate again, there is a clunk from the rear of the car.

80

At other times, under the same condition, I hear a noise similar to that a stick would make as it is dragged along a picket fence. Do you have any ideas on what the cause might be?

The chances are very good that you have a failing universal joint in the drive shaft (Fig. 10-2). Since the noise seems to be coming from the rear of the car, it's reasonable to assume that it is the rear U-joint that is breaking down.

The next time the car is on a lift, have the mechanic check the drive shaft for excessive play. If it shows up, as I suspect it will, you would be well advised to have both the front and rear U-joints replaced since the failure of one often puts excessive strain on the other and it will go sooner or later.

There is a possibility that the clunk is caused by excessive play in the ring and pinion gears inside the rear. In many applications, this can be corrected by the use of shims, but since it's a relatively expensive job, it may not be worth it because it's more of an annoyance than a potential cause for breakdown.

I have a 1975 Chevrolet Blazer which has the new process full-time four-wheel drive. The Blazer came with a 3.01-1 axle ratio, which I would like to change to 4.11-1, which is offered as a option by Chevrolet. I went to the dealer from whom I bought the vehicle and was told that it was only a factory option and that they couldn't help me. I also went through the phone book and couldn't find anyone who would do the change. Do you have any thoughts on the proposal and/or know of anyone who can do it for me?

My initial thought is to forget it, mainly because of the expense involved. A Chevrolet engineer says it could take up to 10 hours labor which, at the average shop price of $15 an hour, is a pretty hefty job. On top of that, you have the cost of two sets of new ring and pinion gears and a speedometer cable (Fig. 10-3). Unless you are going to the rescue of stranded tanks or plan on driving over the absolutely worst terrain imaginable, I think it would be a waste of time, effort, and money. Additionally, you will find that your fuel mileage will be decreased. As for getting the work done, Chevrolet says any of its dealers is capable of doing it but that, since the parts will be special

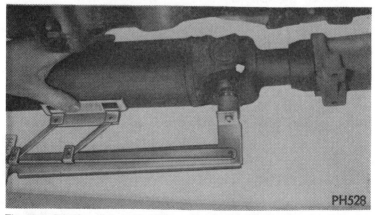

Fig. 10-2. Clunking or thumping on acceleration or deceleration often indicates universal joint failure. This is one test. (Courtesy Chrysler Corp.)

Fig. 10-3. Just about everything you can see inside this differential pumpkin would have to be replaced to change ratio. (Courtesy Chrysler Corp.)

order items, you probably will be asked to put down a hefty deposit upon order.

I have a 1968 Pontiac which, I understand, has sealed bearing on the rear-axle shaft. I would like to know if the bearings could be greased some way if the axles were removed. The car has 55,000 miles on it, and I would like to assure myself that I won't run into bearing failure sometime on a trip. I have been told that they cannot be greased and that you just run them until they fail. Do you have any suggestions?

It seems to me you are making much ado about nothing. Rear-axle bearings are one of the last things to cause trouble in normal circumstances since the weight and pressure on them are constant, unlike front wheel bearings in which the wheels are constantly at a different angle. If you are that much concerned about rear axle bearing failure, I would suggest pulling the axles and replacing the bearings. They certainly don't cost that much.

I bought a 1965 Plymouth and am having trouble with the transmission. When I drive for so many miles it will not go in reverse or will not start in park. After you let it cool, it will be okay. I had the linkage adjusted, had a new filter installed, changed the oil, and had the reverse actuator pump cleaned. I drive to work once a week to keep the oil and working parts okay. I am going to store the car this winter. Do you have any suggestions?

I don't know what the mileage on your car is, but I suspect it's pretty high. I also suspect the fluid never was changed prior to your having it done. As I explained above, old oil has a tendency to gum up like shellac or lacquer

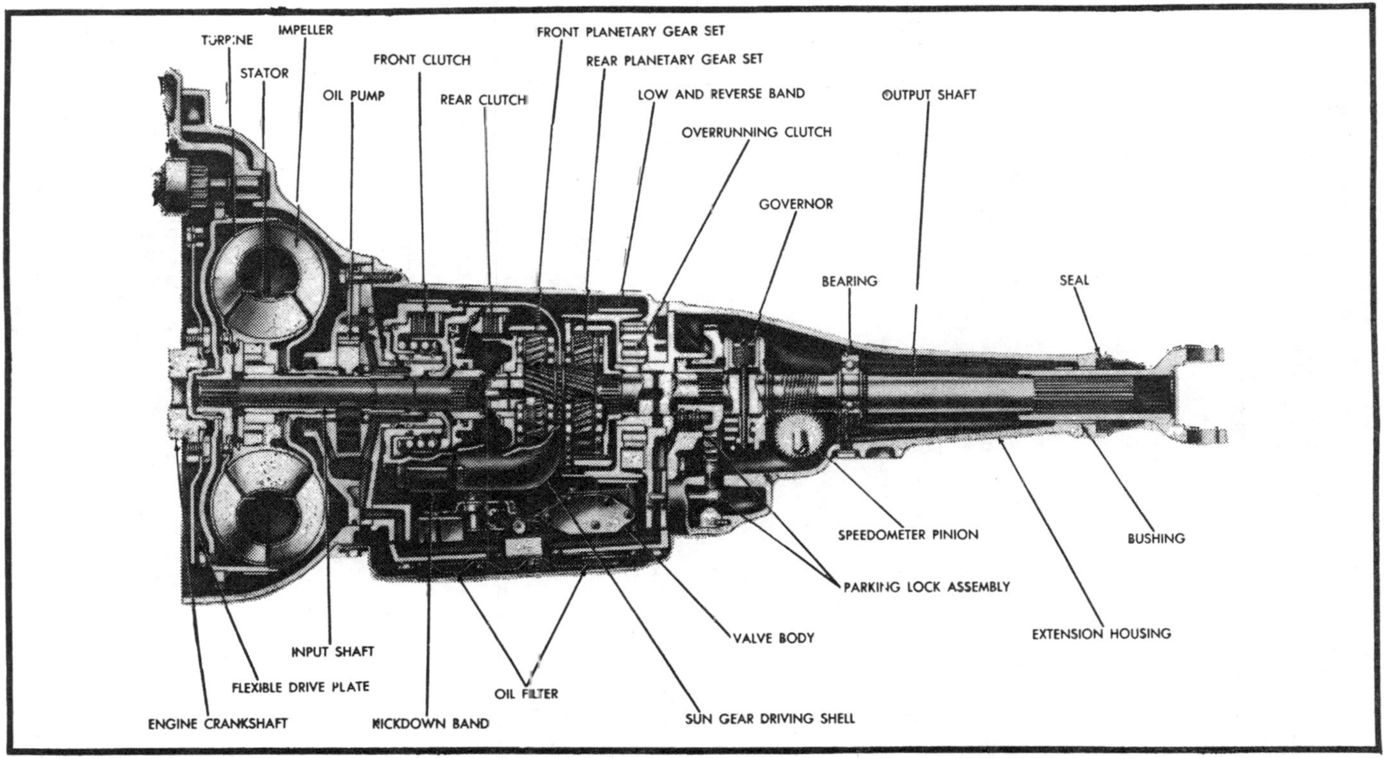
TURBINE
IMPELLER
STATOR
FRONT CLUTCH
OIL PUMP
REAR CLUTCH
FRONT PLANETARY GEAR SET
REAR PLANETARY GEAR SET
LOW AND REVERSE BAND
OVERRUNNING CLUTCH
OUTPUT SHAFT
GOVERNOR
BEARING
SEAL
SPEEDOMETER PINION
BUSHING
PARKING LOCK ASSEMBLY
VALVE BODY
EXTENSION HOUSING
INPUT SHAFT
FLEXIBLE DRIVE PLATE
OIL FILTER
SUN GEAR DRIVING SHELL
ENGINE CRANKSHAFT
KICKDOWN BAND

Fig. 10-4. It's not difficult to understand how gummed-up fluid would have an adverse effect on transmissions. (Courtesy Chrysler Corp.)

and clog various pumps or the valve body (Fig. 10-4). This same situation developed on a 1965 Plymouth Fury that I owned several years ago and it cost me $245 for a rebuilt transmission. (I learned the hard way). Your problem may not be quite as extensive (or expensive), but the transmission will have to be pulled and various pressure tests made to determine the kind and extent of the damage. The work that you had done, unfortunately, probably was too late to help.

I have a 1966 Mustang with a 289 V-8 engine and automatic transmission. I would like to convert to a manual transmission. Can you tell me what I would need to set about such a project and would you advise it?

What you have in mind is like opening the proverbial can of worms. You not only must replace the transmission itself, but everything else between the flywheel and rear axle assembly. That includes the flywheel and driveshaft. Plus you will have to install a clutch and all the operating linkage that goes with it.

If you are intent on doing this, I strongly recommend getting another car from which you can take parts. And in the end, your Mustang will be worth less.

I have a 1975 Chevrolet Impala that has a vibration when it's in a hard pull. It is worse at about 35 mph. This has caused the transmission seals to burst four times, and the car has only 6,000 miles on it. What could be the cause?

Most likely, your problem is a result of one or more bad engine mounts. If this is the case, it permits the engine to move more than is intended and certainly would set up vibrations. Have a mechanic check the condition of both front mounts (on each side of the engine) and the rear mount (under the transmission).

If they check out all right, your trouble could be the result of an out-of-balance drive shaft. That is the long tubular piece that connects the rear of the transmission with the rear axle assembly. At each end of the driveshaft are universal joints which, if bad, could also cause a problem.

I bought a brand new Ford Granada and ran into a problem four or six hours after I picked it up from the dealer. When I went to put it in the garage that evening, I put the gearshift lever in park and went to open the door. When I got back in and went to move the lever to drive, it wouldn't move. I called the salesman and he told me to hold the brake pedal on real hard and pull hard on the lever. It worked. This continues to happen sometimes when the car is parked uphill and sometimes downhill. Can you tell me if this is normal and also about a cracking noise when the engine is started or running at low speeds?

I wouldn't exactly describe your problem as normal, although it is fairly commonplace in cars with automatic transmissions, especially when parking on an incline where the weight of the car is on the park locking device inside the transmission. There is nothing you or a mechanic can do about the situation. If it bothers you excessively, try parking in neutral and holding the car in place with the parking brake.

As for the cracking sound you hear, it probably is due to expansion (caused by heat) of the catalytic converter, which is normal. If you stand around the car after shutting it off, you'll probably hear the same noise, this time caused by contraction as it cools.

I recently purchased a new Chevelle six-cylinder car. On occasion, it would make a loud rumbling noise (like empty tin cans rattling) under the motors.

This noise would come and go. I was told that it was the converter. After one final exceptionally loud rattle, it disappeared and a loud whining noise developed. This high-frequency noise is gradually quieting down but it is constant and still there.

What I would like to know is what it is, and will it affect the car at a future date?

Chevrolet engineers decline to speculate on what your problem may be, although they say it could be any one of a half dozen or so things ranging in repair cost from minimal to fairly substantial.

They also say—very emphatically—that you should take your car in to have this checked. There is a distinct possibility that a minor problem in one area could lead to major ones in another.

Additionally, it is doubtful if the catalytic converter is the item causing the noise since there is nothing in it that could cause the symptoms you describe.

However, one of the major components of an automatic transmission is the torque converter, and it is conceivable that noises similar to that which you describe could be caused by malfunctions there.

No matter, you should have it examined by competent mechanics, especially before your warranty expires.

I have a 1971 Vega with a three-speed manual transmission that is in need of repair. Would it be cheaper to have the transmission fixed or replaced with a used transmission? The car has 50,000 miles on it.

Without knowing exactly what is wrong with your car's transmission, I find it difficult to say which job would be cheaper.

However, when you buy any used part, you must realize that there is always a chance that it is defective. Most reputable parts dealers would guarantee a transmission only to the point of giving you another one should the first one be bad. But you still have the cost of the labor to remove and install.

I suggest getting an estimate on repairing the gearbox you now have, and if it is relatively close to the price of a used one, have the original fixed.

I have a problem with my 1967 Mercury, which has a 390-cubic-inch engine and automatic transmission. When it is cold, the car will not move forward until the engine has run for about 5 minutes. When it is warmed up it runs perfectly. I checked the transmission oil and it is okay. Any suggestions?

When you say the transmission fluid is okay, I am sure you mean it is filled to the proper level. This does not mean it is okay. The chances are that your transmission fluid is breaking down and forming a varnish that is causing your problem.

When cold, this gummy substance will clog various parts of the automatic transmission, impeding or thwarting proper function. As the engine turns the input shafts, the friction of movement gradually warms and thins the fluid until it begins to flow properly.

Unfortunately, many owners never think to have the transmission fluid replaced regularly or to have the filters cleaned or replaced, and this problem is one that keeps many "rebuilders" in business.

At this stage of deterioration, your transmission very well may require a teardown and thorough cleaning. However, you should have it checked promptly to prevent more serious damage.

I own a 1973 Chevelle with six-cylinder engine and standard transmission. My problem is with the gear shift locking and sticking in gear. I can not shift gears unless I raise the hood and loosen the linkage there. One time it locked so badly that I had to loosen it under the car near the transmission.

I had this problem with previous Chevrolets when they reached 80,000 or 90,000 miles, but never with one at 40,000 miles. The dealer readjusted and lubricated the gear (linkage), but it has not solved the problem. Any advice?

Your problem can be caused by one of two things. Most likely, the shifting linkage from the base of the steering column to the side of the transmission has become worn and it jams in position due to the excess play. This can be corrected by replacing the worn linkage. The other possibility is that the shifting forks inside the transmission have been damaged—possibly by forcing it into gear at one time or another (Fig. 10-5). If this is the case, the transmission would have to be removed and torn down, a fairly expensive proposition.

My new Plymouth station wagon developed a leak in the automatic transmission system on a long drive recently. The coupling nut to the transmission oil cooler was cross-threaded. This trouble wasn't diagnosed until after considerable loss of transmission oil with the resultant loss in climbing power.

Since it was a Sunday and I couldn't get service, I had to drive 100 miles back home by periodically adding oil to the transmission. Could there be hidden damage to the transmission even though the leak was fixed? At all times, the dipstick showed some oil although the readings were quite low more than once.

It is very possible that some damage was done, damage that may not show up for 10, 20, even 50,000 miles. And, without completely dismantling the transmission, there is no way to determine the situation.

The chances are very good, however, that you did the transmission no real harm as long as you kept some fluid in it. That is, assuming that it acts as it should now after the repairs have been made.

I would, however, keep a close watch on it. If it begins to make any unusual sounds or shifts at the wrong time, I would get it back to the dealer for repairs—under warranty—before said guarantee runs out.

Even if troubles develop at a later date, you might have a case, but it would be a lot harder to prove. And don't let the receipt get away. It's the only proof you have.

I am a senior citizen and own a 1968 Plymouth with 19,000 miles. Over a year ago, I noticed a slight drip which my serviceman finally located as a slight leak at the transmission pan. He replaced the filter and gaskets, but the leak persists, presently amounting to about 1 pint every four months. Do you think the

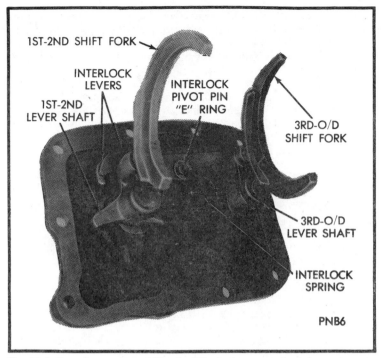

1ST-2ND SHIFT FORK

INTERLOCK
LEVERS

1ST-2ND
LEVER SHAFT

INTERLOCK
PIVOT PIN
"E" RING

3RD-O/D
SHIFT FORK

3RD-O/D
LEVER SHAFT

INTERLOCK
SPRING

PNB6

Fig. 10-5. Sometimes when shifting is difficult, the temptation is to push a little harder on the lever. Bending these shifting forks can be the result. (Courtesy Chrysler Corp).

new gaskets should have stopped the leak entirely or is this something that cannot be avoided and one must live with?

It sounds very much like you may have a leaking transmission seal, possibly in the front, but more likely at the rear where the transmission output shaft is coupled to the drive shaft through a universal joint. Replacement is not all that difficult or expensive, especially when compared to the cost of a major transmission overhaul. It is not at all difficult to check if you have access to a hydraulic lift. First have the car put up on the lift and have the area around the transmission wiped clean. Then take the car on a short run around the neighborhood—10 minutes should be plenty. Bring it back and put it back up on the lift and watch for telltale signs of red fluid. This will pinpoint the area of the leak.

How often should the transmisssion oil be changed? I have a 1966 Buick Electra 225 with 78,000 miles on it, and I don't think the transmission oil has ever been changed.

A good rule of thumb is to change the oil and filter at no more than 50,000 miles. Under heavy use such as regular towing, it should be done at 20,000 miles.

I have a 1970 Mercury with 55,000 miles that I hope to keep for another 50,000 miles. I have never changed the transmission oil on this car or on any of my previous ones. I may have added oil once or twice. My manual says nothing about changing oil, just add it as needed. Do you think changing the oil now might cause any problems? The new oil would be relatively lighter and thinner. Would there be any danger of seals leaking or transmission slipping?

I find it difficult to believe that somewhere in your owner's manual it doesn't indicate a time not only to change the transmission fluid, but to clean or change the filter screen. Most manufacturers, including the Ford Motor Company, recommend this be done at the 25,000-mile mark. In anything like this, there is a 100 percent or better safety factor, which indicates to me that you could be on the near edge of disaster.

As transmission oil gets old and worn through use, especially if it is exposed to extremes of pressure, it will develop a tendency to lacquerize. When this happens, it can clog tiny holes and passages, causing malfunction and necessitating an expensive overhaul. Since having the oil and filter changed is about a $20 job, I'd call it cheap insurance.

I have a 1974 Mustang II, automatic with a V-6 engine. Since the car has a tach, I should be able to use the tach wisely to improve my mileage (power is secondary to me, so I drive slowly, carefully, and wisely).

First, can you tell me how to use the tach for better mileage, and can you tell me anything about efficiency curves (of the engine) which I can use along with the tach?

Without getting deeply embroiled in a technical explanation of automatic transmissions, let me say that if you currently drive slowly and carefully, there is a little more that you could do to improve the car's fuel mileage.

Torque and efficiency curves (which show where you get the most usable power and economy through the engine's operating range) can be of considerable help in a car with standard transmission. However, an automatic transmission is set to shift at the optimum point of engine rpms, and if you use the other ranges to vary these shift points, you'll probably decrease your mileage.

Then why the tachometer you ask? In this application, it is more for show than anything else. The Mustang II is a sporty little car, and a tachometer on the dashboard adds to that flair.

I have a 1975, 8-cylinder, Mustang II Ghia with 20,800 miles, and on occasion the transmission will not shift from second to drive (high or third gear). After some manipulation by shifting to neutral and revving the engine, it will return to drive for awhile, then shift to second again. Eventually it returns to drive and operates properly.

This occurs in the morning and was constant during the cold weather. Now, it does not occur every day. Two mechanics have tested the car, but apparently the condition did not show up for them. The transmission was serviced at 17,000 miles. What is your evaluation?

I hate to be vague, but your problem could be caused by something as simple as low fluid level or incorrect linkage adjustment or a half dozen internal problems that can require an overhaul. That's if it's the transmission. Sometimes late shifts can be caused by engine problems. An engine that is out of tune (it could be affected by choke problems in the cold) or one with mechanical problems such as low compression will produce less torque at high-throttle openings and low manifold vacuum levels. Since the transmission reacts to either manifold vacuum or throttle position, an abnormal engine will adversely affect the transmission.

Also, you said you had the transmission services but didn't elaborate. That job should include draining the fluid, removing, cleaning, and replacing the filter, and installing new fluid. If all that wasn't done, fluid failure could cause your problems.

At any rate, I'm sure the situation will not get better by itself, and you'd be well advised to have it fixed before something more serious occurs.

Chapter 11
Gas, Oil, and Additives

Can you tell me if there is a difference in the gasoline sold at the major oil company stations and the so-called independent stations? We are having a lot of trouble with a rough-running engine. A tune-up didn't help. For instance, at times you can floor the gas pedal and just get up to a speed of 20 mph and, all of a sudden, the car will take off. My husband insists it's the gas and if we paid as much as 17 cents a gallon more for the major company gas, the car would operate all right. He seems to think the cheaper gas gums up the carburetor.

The gasoline sold at independent stations is no more likely to be "bad" than that sold under name brands. In fact, it often comes from the same refinery—being sold to the independent retailer in bulk form. I would suggest that you buy several tankfuls from a different retailer to see if the problem doesn't clear up. If not, I would recommend having your car's entire fuel system checked—from possible dirt in the tank through the fuel pump and filter to the carburetor.

I own a 1970 Ford Maverick. Recently, I stopped at a service station and asked for regular gas. As I got out of the car to pay the attendant, I noticed the gas was unleaded.

Since that time, the car has been hard to start in the morning and cuts off at nearly every stop. It idles roughly and there's been a loss of power on acceleration. Any ideas?

I suspect that you have trouble in the car's fuel system, but I don't believe it is the fault of the unleaded regular gas. Most likely the culprit is either the carburetor or the fuel pump.

Our 1967 Dodge van has a problem with gas vapor. When the motor is stopped, the passenger compartment fills with heavy fumes. It is worse in warm weather, but happens in the cold as well. Various mechanics have given a wide variety of suggestions but can't agree on an effective solution. Attempted remedies include special attention to various valves (heat risers, etc.) and a "mile-master pressure regulator" on the gas line to the carburetor. No success. Can you suggest anything?

I would take a long, hard look at the carburetor to see if fuel is seeping out of various joints (Fig. 11-1). If so, it would evaporate when hitting the manifold and cause the fumes you describe. This could be caused by any number of things from bad gaskets to a damaged float chamber valve. Another possibility is insufficient cooling, which would permit fuel remaining in the carburetor after the engine is turned off to "percolate." It then would be a gaseous vapor. As a stop-gap measure, I would remove the engine cover and replace all the seals around it in an attempt to keep the fumes from seeping into the passenger compartment. I would do this anyway, because if the seals are bad enough to allow gasoline vapors to seep in, they certainly wouldn't stop carbon monoxide in the event of an exhaust system leak.

Does fuel with no lead, some lead, and lots of lead mix in my tank or burn separately like that good old drink called a Horse's Neck?

Fig. 11-1. Many times screws work loose to the point that gasoline can seep through at carburetor joints, causing fumes. (Courtesy AMC)

Gasolines with different lead content mix like a Harvey Wallbanger. Just the pressure of the flow coming into the tank is enough to mix things thoroughly.

I am the owner of a Chevrolet Nova with a 350-cubic-inch V-8 engine. The owner's manual says I should use unleaded gasoline with an octane rating of 91 or better.

My problem is that I cannot find octane with this rating anywhere. Could you tell me if there is such a gas?

Yes, there is such a gas, known as premium unleaded, available at selected service stations across the country. However, you do not need this type of fuel.

The confusion arises over the fact that there are two methods to measure the octane rating of fuel, called research and motor. The figures they arrive at—through similar, but distinctly different test methods—are roughly four points apart.

What is rated at 91 octane by one method actually is 87 octane by the other. This is the fuel that Chevrolet had in mind when it published the figure that is in your owner's manual.

In recent months, steps have been taken to post on the pumps an average of the two ratings. Therefore, most of the fuel is rated at either 89 or 90 octane, which is where the problem lies. Many motorists such as yourself are faced with the same dilemma.

What it means is that cars that are recommended to run on "91 octane" fuel are meant to run on everyday regular unleaded fuel that is available at just about every station.

Some prankster poured sugar in the gas tanks of both of my cars. Can you tell me what is happening or will happen to my engine? What should I do to prevent possible damage?

From the way your question is worded, I doubt if your not-so-practical jokester put very much sugar in the tanks. Otherwise, it wouldn't be very long at all before the sweet stuff made things very sour for your cars.

Sugar in a car's fuel system will foul everything it comes in contact with—especially the carburetor. I wouldn't advise using the cars until you get things cleaned out.

If the engines haven't been run, the cleaning procedure involves removing the fuel tanks and flushing them thoroughly with water to remove all foreign substances. If the cars have been started, everything from the tanks to the carburetors will have to be dismantled (Fig. 11-2) and cleaned. Even the slightest residue can result in nagging problems at a later date.

Fortunately, incidents like this are becoming more infrequent. But as long as there is the remotest possibility of some joker trying it, this is one of the best reasons in the world for a locking gas cap.

I have been putting Magnus Chemical (gasoline additive) in my cars for more than 30 years. Since I've never had a frozen gas line or burned valve in any car, I would like to continue using the product. However, I recently bought a 1975 Plymouth Valiant with a catalytic converter. I'd like to know if I can continue to use the additive or if doing so would be harmful to the converter.

There are some gasoline additives that do not contain lead and can be used without fear of causing damage. I am not familiar with Magnus Chemi-

Fig. 11-2. When you start to dismantle fuel system, one of the first steps (after disconnecting the battery) is to pump out the tank. (Courtesy Chrysler Corp.)

cal, but one that I know is safe is Wynn's X-Tend Gas Treatment. Also, STP Gas Treatment has been certified as safe, but that company recommends against pouring the additive straight through the carburetor for a quick cleanout. If used this way, moist additives will cause enough hot spots to damage the catalyst. Incidentally, the overwhelming majority of these products have their ingredients listed on the label. Any that list lead should be avoided.

I have two questions that relate to the 1975 Vega station wagon that I bought in June of 1975. At that time, I was told it has a (5-year) 60,000 mile-warranty on the engine. I never received a printed warranty from the Chevrolet people but the dealer promised I was covered. Is this true or can I expect trouble if engine problems develop?

Also, I have had to add one quart of oil every 500 miles like clockwork. The dealer's mechanic said this was normal for this car with the aluminum engine and catalytic converter. Is this true?

As far as the warranty is concerned, you should have nothing to worry about. The only thing that determines whether the car is still in warranty is the odometer reading (they, of course, can tell if it's been tampered with and that would nullify the warranty).

From the sound of your second question, it would appear that engine problems have already developed. Neither the fact that it has an aluminum engine nor that it is equipped with a catalytic converter should have any bearing whatsoever on whether it uses oil or not.

Assuming you have mileage somewhere in the normal range (10,000 to 15,000 miles per year), there is no way that your car's engine should be consuming oil at the rate of a quart every 500 miles. More normal would be a quart between recommended oil changes.

If I were you, I'd insist that the oil consumption problem be corrected under warranty. If you get no satisfaction from the mechanic or service manager, insist on seeing the dealer and complain to him. If you are still dissatisfied, contact your regional zone office of Chevrolet and insist that a factory representative inspect the car. Chevrolet claims it is most anxious to correct such problems.

Can anyone define acceptable oil consumption? My 1973 Audi Fox got about 1,200 miles to a quart of oil for its first 15,000 miles. Oil consumption increased to 250 miles per quart by the 20,000 mile mark at which time the dealer installed new valve guides under warranty. Also at that time, a compression check revealed one cylinder at 40 pounds, the others at 150.

Immediately thereafter, consumption dropped to 500 miles per quart, then reverted to about 250 miles per quart after about 4,000 miles. The car now has 58,000 miles on it and consumes about a quart every 200 miles.

You obviously have ring or cylinder wall damage (Fig. 11-3) in the cylinder that has the low reading. To be sure, you might have another compression test done and after the original test, have the mechanic squirt some oil in the bad cylinder. If the pressure rises, this is indicative of worn rings (if not, it would indicate valve problems).

At the point you have reached, you have one of three choices. You could have the engine torn down for inspection and replacement of the piston rings if that's where the trouble is. If the cylinder wall is scored badly enough, that could necessitate a new block. Either way, it'd be very expensive because as long as it's apart, it would be foolish not the replace bearings and have a valve job done.

You could continue adding oil as needed and try a can of STP or other similar heavy additive to increase the oil velocity. This often cuts oil consumption.

Lastly, you could start buying cheap oil in bulk, add when necessary, and run it into the ground. Unfortunately, the latter course wouldn't take very long to accomplish.

As to oil consumption, the general rule is that an engine should consume about a quart of oil every 2,500 miles or so. But there will be variations to a slight degree.

I have a six-cylinder 1974 Plymouth Valiant with 24,000 miles on it. I change oil and filter every 3,000 miles or three

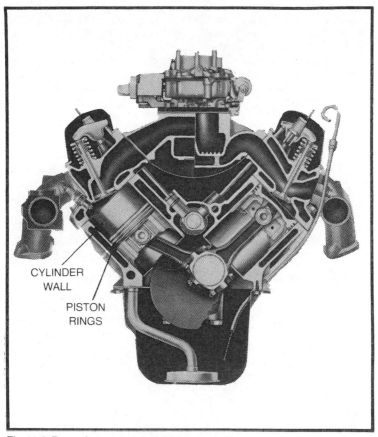

CYLINDER
WALL

PISTON
RINGS

Fig. 11-3. Excessive wear to piston rings or cylinder walls will reduce the seal and increase oil consumption. (Courtesy Chrysler Corp.)

months. When I do this job, it only takes four quarts of oil although the manual says it requires five quarts.

When I check the dipstick, it shows full and the warning light for oil pressure on the dashboard never lights up, so I assume that it doesn't need oil. Can you tell me why it shows full after only adding four quarts of oil?

I suspect that you are checking the dipstick after adding the four quarts of fresh oil and before running the engine. This would tend to give the results you describe because the new oil hasn't had a chance to circulate and build up in the new filter.

If you check the oil level after running the engine, I think you'll find the level has dropped to the point that you could use most of another quart of oil. This system is intended for checks shortly after the engine has been turned off (most checks are done by service station attendants during gas stops). I don't think you're hurting the engine by running a quart low, but you are eliminating a built-in safety factor.

I have a 1954 Plymouth that uses regular oil in the engine. Could I switch to a detergent oil or would I cause any serious damage to the motor?

I definitely advise against using detergent oil in an engine that has run for 22 years on nondetergent oil. The reason is that the sludge and carbon buildups (that detergent oil will constantly flush from an engine) are there in considerable quantities. If you should switch to a detergent oil now, it wouldn't be very long before all these deposits are flushed away, leaving excess wear areas in which oil can seep into the combustion chambers. This would result in an engine that would puff smoke all the time and possibly consume upwards of a quart of oil every 100 miles or so.

I have a 1972 Volvo 144-E with automatic transmission. I purchased the car used and was informed by the previous owner that he had used only high-quality nondetergent oil in the engine and that he had changed the oil faithfully every 2,000 miles.

I have been advised to switch to detergent multi-viscosity oil. Are there advantages to doing this? Is it possible that the cleaning action of the detergent oil could plug things up with the settled gunk?

What about oil use? Is it likely I could use much less oil by switching to detergent oil or would that be temporary?

Not too long ago, I advised the owner of a 1969 Camaro with 75,000 miles on it not to switch from nondetergent to detergent oil. I said that I felt that detergent oils will tend to clean out sludge buildups from the other oil and could cause increased oil consumption.

An Exxon representative responded to that by saying that I am perpetuating an old wives' tale. It is, he said, Exxon's position that nondetergent oils not be used in anything except "bicycles and roller skates." He claims that detergent oils will not clean out deposits left by nondetergent oil. Rather, it will only prevent any additional buildup.

He added that there are very few high-quality nondetergent oils on the market and that motorists in such situations would be advised to use a top-quality multi-viscosity detergent oil, changing both the oil and filter at factory specified intervals.

I'm not so sure, especially in high-mileage cars in which there is no documented evidence of the frequency of maintenance.

However, I do agree with him that high-quality nondetergent oils are becoming more and more scarce, both in the number of manufacturers and in availability.

With your car that has had frequent changes of both oil and filter by an owner who obviously cared, I wouldn't worry about switching over. In the long run, I think you'd be better off.

And I wouldn't be concerned about the sediment gunking things up because the detergent additives in oil don't work that way. Simply stated, the detergents keep the foreign particles suspended in the oil so that when you drain your oil, they are flushed out of the engine.

It's true that the oil may pick up some sludge, mainly that which has accumulated in the botton of the sump. For that reason, you might be advised to change oil and filter more often than recommended the first couple of times.

As for increased consumption, that won't happen unless the engine is severely worn. If it does occur, it will not be temporary.

I own a 1974 Cadillac with 8,000 miles on it and plan to start using a synthetic oil. What do you think of these products? I read the complete history of synthetic oils in a magazine and it sounds all right to me.

As far as I am concerned, the jury is still out on synthetic oils. My only objection to them is the fact that they are so expensive—$3.95 a quart of Mobil 1, which is the best known and the only one yet to be marketed by a major oil company.

It has been proven in laboratory and practical applications that synthetics can last up to 30,000 or more miles between changes. That would make them economically feasible.

But Mobil makes no such claims as these (if it did, it might wind up at the very least having to defend a lot of consumer claims). And, although the auto manufacturers have given tacit approval for the use of synthetics in their cars, they still require oil changes at recommended intervals, on the average about every 5,000 miles.

Although Mobil claims its synthetic oil will give you slightly better gasoline mileage because of reduced friction, it would be difficult if not impossible to make up the difference between that $3.95 and the $1.50 a quart that is the maximum for most premium oils.

I was reading in an auto accessory catalog about a synthetic motor oil called EON E-11 that is thermally stable from minus 60 degrees to 600 degrees. It also claims to give from 20,000 to 40,000 miles between oil changes.

I have a 1970 Pontiac LeMans with a 350 V-8 engine, and I change the oil every 3,000 miles with a commercial 10-40 oil. The car has 70,000 miles on it. I also have a 1968 Chevy with a 307 that burns a little oil.

Can I use this synthetic motor oil in either one of my cars without any damage to the engines? Also, could all their claims be true? The oil lists for $24.99 for a case of six quarts.

I know of no reason that you couldn't use a synthetic oil in any automotive lubrication situation. However, if you intend to go 20,000 or 40,000 miles between oil changes, make sure that there is an unconditional warranty against engine damage.

These synthetics have gone that far—even as much as 50,000 miles—without a change under laboratory-controlled tests. But I know of no synthetic oil manufacturer who is offering an iron-clad guarantee.

Therefore, if you're going to have to change oil regularly anyhow, it would seem difficult to justify more than $4 a quart for the oil.

I am having a disagreement with my son-in-law about the type of oil he uses in his 1975 Buick. Ever since he got the car new, he has been using nondetergent oil of good quality in the car. I say he is wrong because he has a high-compression engine and it needs a high-detergent oil.

He also uses the same oil in my daughter's 1969 Ford Falcon. Can you settle this for me?

First off, the engine in a 1975 Buick is not what we have come to accept as high-compression. Most engines in recent years, and almost all built since

1975, have been relatively low in compression as a part of the fight against air pollution.

But, even if it were a high-compression engine, this would have no bearing on the use of nondetergent or high-detergent oil. When fresh, both types of oil (of the same grade and SAE viscosity rating) have equal lubricating properties. The difference is that as dirt accumulates in the engine through normal operation, the detergent oil will keep it "suspended" and when you change oil, the majority of the impurities will wash out with the old oil. With nondetergent oil, these particles will build up sludge over the years, causing excess wear and eventually getting to the point that oil changes becomes useless.

I own a 1970 Chevrolet Malibu that has approximately 70,000 miles on it. The engine is a V-8 with two-barrel carburetor. The transmission is in excellent condition, and the heater and air conditioner work fine.

My only complaint is that I seem to have to add oil every 100 miles or so. There are no oil leaks, no smoke from the exhaust, and no odd or disturbing smells. I've been seriously thinking of buying another car but money is a bit tight right now.

The Malibu gets about 15 – 17 miles per gallon with excellent pickup. What can be my problem and would it be worth getting fixed?

Your letter leaves me in something of a quandary. There are only three ways that oil can get out of an engine—through a leak, burning, or being deliberately removed. If there is a leak, it almost always is visible and, since you are using a quart every 100 miles, it certainly would be. Some types of slow leaks occasionally occur only when the engine is running and can be very difficult to spot, but not at the rate you are losing it.

If the car is burning oil—due either to bad rings or bad valve seals—this also would be highly visible at a rate of 100 miles to the quart. It is possible that you don't recognize what you are seeing. Oil burning is most visible upon starting, in hard acceleration and often on deceleration. Run your finger around the inside of the exhaust pipe (when it's cold, of course) and if you come away with a very dirty finger, chances are you're burning oil.

As to whether it would be worth it to have the car fixed, it's difficult to say. Depending on what the trouble is, it could cost you anywhere from $20 to repair a leaky pan gasket up to $250 or so if you need new rings.

I would like to know if the additives you add to your oil to help stop a light tapping will hurt the engine in any way. Can you recommend a good additive to help stop the tapping?

All the major-brand additives that claim to help in quieting noisy lifters will prove effective in most cases. However, your engine got into that state only through neglect, be it accidental or deliberate. The reason for the tapping is that the hydraulic lifters (Fig. 11-4) that ride between the camshaft lobes and pushrods have become clogged with sludge and no longer absorb the shocks they are intended to do.

If engine oil and filter are changed at recommended intervals, this condition will never develop. Incidentally, a few engines in older cars have solid lifters, in which case, the only way to cure the tapping is to adjust the rocker arms.

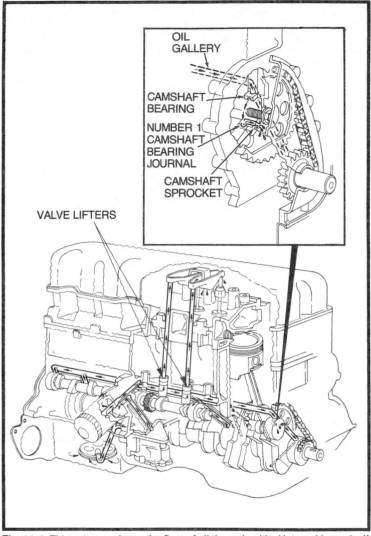

OIL GALLERY

CAMSHAFT BEARING

NUMBER 1 CAMSHAFT BEARING JOURNAL

CAMSHAFT SPROCKET

VALVE LIFTERS

Fig. 11-4. This cutaway shows the flow of oil through critical internal journals. If the oil isn't changed regularly, dirty oil will clog the hydraulic lifters. (Courtesy AMC)

My car manual says to change the oil and filter every 6,000 miles or six months, whichever comes first. My oil and filter has only between 2,500 and 3,000 miles on it at the end of six months. Why is it necessary to change oil and filter if it has only that small amount of mileage on it? Isn't this a waste of oil?

Any significant use is enough to institute chemical changes in the oil which lead to its gradual decomposition. Generally speaking, oil with 3,000 miles on it will be in about the same condition as oil with 6,000 miles—

needing a change. The same, of course, holds true for the filter since, if you change oil without replacing the filter, you'll just be contaminating the new oil.

Once and for all, can you tell me if oil additives of the type you buy at a gas station or local auto store help an engine run better, smoother, last longer, or produce better mileage?

The answer is yes, no, and maybe, depending on who you talk to. Auto manufacturers as well as independent rebuilders and many mechanics, although not condemning their use, do not encourage it. In fact, one of the East Coast's major engine rebuilders says that such products actually can harm the engine. Here's the problem: When the engine isn't running, the additives separate from the oil. When the engine is started, the oil intake pipe may be surrounded by the thick additive, which can impede the flow of oil and actually increase wear.

On the positive side, STP, the largest manufacturer of such products, has documented proof that under hard and continuous operation, its "Oil Treatment" does reduce wear. This is especially true under warm or hot-weather conditions.

STP and like products also can be of great value in older worn engines where oil consumption and low oil pressure are major factors. For example, several years ago, I purchased a used (and abused) Jaguar XK120 that got about 100 miles to a quart of oil and had about 20 pounds of oil pressure. Two cans of STP added to the 12-quart sump increased pressure to 60 pound and decreased consumption to a quart every 700 miles or so.

As a rule of thumb, these aftermarket products can be of help in warm weather use and when sustained operation is the rule. In cold weather or short-run operation of cars in generally good condition, they probably won't be of help.

I have a 1954 Customline V-8 Ford. I have owned it for three months. It is in good condition. I would like to know if I could use a 30-weight oil in this car in the winter. It has been on 20-weight nondetergent oil in the past and I am having a hard time finding a dealer or gas station that sells that type of oil. I've been told that since the car has never had detergent oil, a change would cause problems now.

In a moderate climate, you probably can get away with using a 30-weight oil. If it were much colder, you would run into problems because the oil would congeal to such a degree that starting might be difficult, if not impossible.

Most oil companies still offer a 20-weight nondetergent oil, although most retail outlets limit stock to a small amount if they carry it at all. This is because the overwhelming preponderance of vehicles now on the road use multi-viscosity, high-detergent oils.

You are absolutely correct in not using a detergent oil because, over the years, carbon builds up as sludge on internal engine surfaces and, when a detergent oil is introduced, it eventually will clean these deposits away resulting in anything from increased oil consumption to eventual engine failure.

The threads on my oil plug are stripped. I am losing a little oil. What can I do, short of buying and installing a new oil pan?

Assuming you mean the threads in the drain hole are stripped, you can shop around for a slightly larger plug then, using a matching tap, cut new threads in the pan to accept it.

I just bought a 1969 Camero with a 350 engine and two-barrel carburetor. There are 75,000 miles on the car, but the engine seems to be in good condition.

I would like to know if I can use regular gasoline instead of premium in this engine and what is the recommended type of engine oil for it?

Let me answer the easy part first. In your area, where temperatures rarely dip to the freezing mark, I would say that a good quality 20W-40 oil would suit your purposes. This would give you relative thinness for starting purposes, increasing to 40W to combat the ravages of heat. Were you located in a colder area where even thinner oil is recommended for starting, the 10W-40 would be best.

One word of caution. If the previous owner has been using nondetergent oil or failed to change the oil at normal intervals, there will be buildups of carbon and sludge which a high-detergent oil will clean out, causing oil consumption problems. If that is the case, you'd be advised to use nondetergent oil.

As to your fuel, that engine has a 9-to-1 compression ratio which is on the borderline between low and high compression. Generally speaking, it should run properly on a regular fuel.

If, however, your discover a pinging noise on acceleration that would indicate pre-ignition (or knock, as it's called), switch over to premium. In many cases like this, an occasional tankful of premium between those of regular are enough to eliminate the problem.

I have a 1939 Mercury sedan that's driving me up a wall. I have just installed a new fuel pump at the recommendation of a reputable mechanic. Still, I am getting gasoline pumped into the oil pan. I can drain the crankcase, put in only two quarts of oil (it holds four), and after about 30 minutes of driving time, the dipstick shows full (gas, of course).

Any suggestions?

Assuming the new fuel pump is in good working order (fuel leaking into the crankcase is caused by a cracked diaphragm), the only other possibility is down the cylinder walls. This can happen, especially in older cars with lower-compression engines, without being really noticeable. What happens is that at least one plug isn't firing. It could be caused by fouling of the plug itself, by a broken ignition wire, or by a broken connector in the distributor cap.

What happens is that the fuel that enters that cylinder washes down the walls and into the crankcase.

The reason you might not notice it is that engine compression (it was 6.15-to-1 when new) is further reduced by years of use. In a newer high-compression engine, a nonfiring plug would be clearly evident as a miss. The way to check is to run the engine for a few minutes, then shut it off and pull the plugs. The ones that aren't firing will be very obvious: they will be soaking wet. Then trace them back to discover why they aren't firing and make the repair.

Whatever you do, don't run it in that condition. The lack of lubrication will very quickly score the cylinder walls and, at the least, you'll face a reboring job.

Chapter 12
Suspension

I own a 1972 Cadillac that was always serviced at the dealership. Recently during a long trip, I pulled into a service station for a lube job. I was informed that it could not be done as there were no fittings, only plugs. They advised me to replace the fittings so that the car could be greased. Otherwise, I would be in for serious trouble.

The Cadillac dealer advised against this, saying the car does not need a grease job for 25,000 miles (there are 19,000 on the car now).

The dealer seems to be every bit as opposed to doing this as the independent mechanics are for it. What's your opinion?

As much as I hate to go against General Motors (because their engineers undoubtedly know more than I do and they'll give me 500 reasons why I'm wrong), I would have the fittings installed (Fig. 12-1).

My 1975 Plymouth Scamp started making a scraping, vibrating noise when I started it after it had sat for long periods such as overnight. It makes this noise for five or six blocks and then stops. When I take it to the mechanic, he tells me he'll have to hear it, but by the time I get there, it's gone. I also had a thumping noise that was cured by replacing a wheel bearing, but now it's starting the same thing again. Any suggestions?

Like your mechanic, I can't tell what is causing your scraping, vibrating noise without hearing it. But I will tell you to get it looked at as soon as possible before some permanent damage results. You should make an appointment with your mechanic to leave the car overnight so he can check it out first thing the next morning. As for your wheel bearing problem, it sounds as though you probably have a bad spindle or wheel hub (which are the surfaces between which the bearing runs). Either or both will have to be replaced to effect a permanent cure.

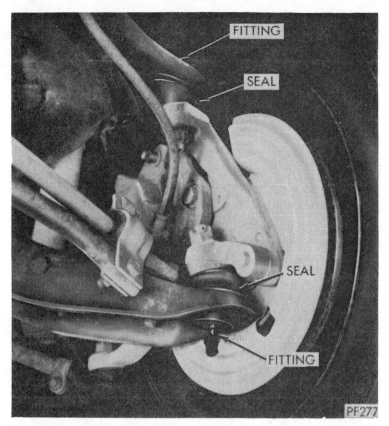

FITTING

SEAL

SEAL

FITTING

PF277

Fig. 12-1. Among the most crucial lubrication points on any automobile are the upper and lower ball joints. (Courtesy Chrysler Corp.)

I have restored a 1968 Cadillac Sedan deVille, spending a considerable amount of money on such things as a new driveshaft, rebuilt transmission, extensive front-end and engine work, a new paint job, vinyl roof, new shock absorbers, new front and rear springs, and new four-ply polyglas tires. On a straightaway, this car rides like a dream. But going across small holes or bumps, it bangs like a truck instead of a luxury car. Do you have any idea what I might try next?

The only suggestion I can offer is to back over what you did before— especially in the area of springs and shock absorbers. Several years ago I got involved in the restoration of a Jaguar roadster and had a spring company build new rear springs for the car. Afterward, it was the harshest riding thing you ever saw. If either your new springs or shocks are rated too stiffly, an extremely harsh ride will result.

I own a 1974 Dodge Dart Custom four-door sedan that sits cockeyed. That is to say it goes down the street in a sideways manner as if the frame is out of line. I had the car to an alignment shop to have the wheels aligned and the torsion bars adjusted—to no avail. The people there advised me to take the car to a shop that specializes in frame alignment, where I was told that the car has the wrong rear in it. My Dodge dealer, however, tells me that the rear is the correct one. As a result, I am wearing out tires at less than 20,000 miles and get terrible gasoline mileage—12 miles per gallon in the city and 15 on the highway. To be honest, I don't know which way to turn and would be very thankful if you could advise me.

To start with, I doubt very much if you have the "wrong" rear in the car. There are several rear-axle ratios available in every model American car, and if you bought your car off the showroom floor as most people do, you could have gotten any one of them. From your description of mileage, I would say you have a high-ratio axle—which should give you excellent acceleration. By the same token, it will adversely affect your mpg, especially at highway speeds. And, considering you have a V-8 built in the last year of restrictive tuning to control emissions, 12 to 15 miles per gallon doesn't sound all that bad.

It is distinctly possible that the rear-axle assembly is improperly mounted—an inch in either direction on either side would result in "crablike" operation of the vehicle.

For a simple check, take a long tape measure and check the distance between the centers of the front and rear wheels on one side, then the other. They should be the same—exactly. If you find any discrepancy, as I suspect you will, take the car to a shop that specializes in repair and replacement of springs to have the rear axle remounted properly.

I have a 1974 Ford Ranch Wagon and find I am always fighting to keep it in a straight line. I'm driving along and it seems to go right or left without me steering it in either direction. My dealer put in new shocks and claims the (steering) gear box is all right. Since the car passed inspection, it's not that it isn't safe. I just don't feel comfortable driving under these conditions.

Since you have had new shock absorbers installed and the steering box is in good order, you must check other areas of the front suspension. The most likely culprits are the idler arm or tie rod ends (Fig. 12-2). The idler arm acts as a dummy steering box on the right side of the car. It is the point where the steering linkage is attached to the right side of the frame at a point corresponding to the location of the steering box on the left. When it begins to wear, it shows up as excessive play.

The tie rod ends are adjustable joints on the ends of the rod used to link the left and right front wheels together. Damage in this area will cause either or both to wander.

The front end of my 1972 Toyota Corolla shimmies very badly when I go over a rough road at more than 30 miles per hour. I took the car to a dealer and he told me the entire front end suspension needed rebuilding. I went to another garage and the mechanic tightened a stud going into the steering gear box. This helped for about 500 miles. The car is shimmying again, and the garage mechanic wants to replace the steering gear assembly. Can you tell me if the second guy got lucky or was the first guy correct?

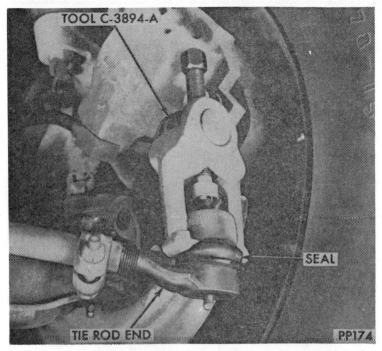

Fig. 12-2. Excessive wear in the tie rods will cause undue play in a car's steering system. A clamp-like tool is a help in replacement. (Courtesy Chrysler Corp.)

It sounds very much like the second guy was right on the money as far as your problem was concerned. What often happens is that a seal goes in the steering box and, as the lubricant gradually escapes, excess wear is caused. The stud you refer to (Fig. 12-3) is an adjusting screw that actually shims up the gearing inside the box and cuts down on the amount of "play" in the steering assembly. There is, of course, a point at which no further adjustment is possible and a new steering gear unit is required.

Should a 1974 Dodge Swinger, properly greased, require new lower ball joints at 24,000 miles? A friend who is trying to sell me the car contends that it's a Chrysler weakness. Is it, or should regular lubrication have prevented this?

Your friend is wrong. There are no inherent weaknesses in ball joints of Chrysler (or any other major brand) cars. If there were, safety reasons would have forced a recall campaign long before this. That is not to say there could not be an isolated instance.

But I am inclined to believe the car rarely was lubricated. This is not to condemn your friend because it is very possible he might have been ripped off. More times than most of us realize, an inexperienced mechanic may do a lube job hitting only the grease fittings he sees and ignoring those out of the way.

In the winter, my 1967 Mustang squeaks like an old baby buggy. It seems to be worse when the weather is bad. What can be done to overcome this problem?

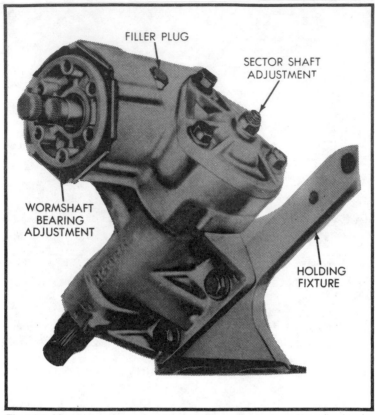

Fig. 12-3. Many times, excessive steering play can be corrected by adjusting the sector shaft screw. It can be a sign of worse things to come, often necessitating steering gear replacement. (Courtesy Chrysler Corp.)

Your car probably is afflicted with an ailment that seems to plague many older models—especially Ford products—that are exposed to extremes of heat and cold.

The problem probably lies in those suspension joints that aren't supposed to need lubrication. The most likely spot is the bushings where the front suspension's upper A-arms attach to the frame. To affect a permanent cure, the bushings must be replaced—a rather extensive job.

It is possible to quiet these bushings down by loosening the large retaining nuts and spraying the area well with a silicone lubricant. This will have to be repeated once or twice a year.

It is possible that other "sealed" fittings are causing the problem. A good soaking with the same type of lubricant should quiet things down.

The front of my 1972 Ford Torino (eight-cylinder engine with air conditioning and power steering) is so low to the ground that it hits stop blocks in parking lots and scrapes the ground when entering off-street driveways that other automobiles use without any trouble.

On even a slightly rough road the ride is very poor with hard, loud thumps and bumps. New shock absorbers have been installed with no appreciable improvement. What further steps can I take to eliminate the situation?

It sounds very much like your front springs are weak and need to be replaced. On rare occasions, springs of the wrong rating are installed at the factory. Most of the time, however, they begin to sag as the car's mileage builds up.

All the symptoms you describe, especially the rough ride and loud thumping noises, are indicative of weak front springs. The rough ride is caused by the loss of spring effect while the thumping noises are a result of decreased travel of the springs.

Shock absorbers, by the way, are misnamed. They should be called shock dampers as they are in England. What they do is hydraulically stop the bouncing caused by the springs on impact of the wheels with road bumps.

Your local dealer could install new stock springs or you might want to contact a shop that specializes in springs and suspension systems. Depending on use, your car might need springs of different rate than stock.

I have a 1974 Olds Delta 88 with 2,700 miles on it. The left front vibrates beginning at 50 miles per hour and gets worse at 60 mph. The left front tire became cupped due to the vibration.

I have had new shocks installed, had new front tires put on and balanced, removed the front wheels and the bearings checked out. I also had the front end aligned. It still vibrates. Can you offer any solution?

Assuming that the people who installed and balanced your new tires also inflated them to the proper pressure, there are other areas that could cause the problem.

Fig. 12-4. One of the first areas to check for excessive play is the steering gear arm and the idler arm. (Courtesy Chrysler Corp.)

First, it might be an eccentric brake disc on the left front wheel. This would serve to throw the whole wheel assembly out of balance and cause vibration.

More likely, it could be worn or loose steering linkage (Fig. 12-4) at any point back to the box at the base of the steering column. This should show up in an alignment but you'd be surprised at how often something like that can get by, especially on a car with mileage as low as yours.

Lastly, the vibration could be caused by a weak spring and the vibration, in turn, could cause the cupping of the tire. Should this be the case, both front springs should be replaced, not just the weak one.

One other remote possibility is a wheel that is bent so slightly as to not be visible to the naked eye. That should show up in dynamic balancing.

I have a 1971 Capri with 73,000 miles. On a slight right turn, a bad vibration develops in the whole car. Nothing has helped including new radial tires, balancing, etc. Any suggestions will be appreciated.

The first thing I would check is the condition of both the front wheel bearing and the spindles. The problem probably is on the left side since it absorbs the pressure on right-hand turns.

Should these check out all right, I would check for excessive play in the front wheels, which would indicate wear in anything from the steering to the suspension. If there is excessive play, any front-end specialist should be able to trace the problem.

Other possibilities include weak shock absorbers or springs or even a bent wheel.

My car, a 1968 Chrysler station wagon, has worn out two sets of tires on the rear just like they do on the front when it is in need of alignment. They wear just on the side.

Can you tell me what is wrong and what I can do?

There are a few possibilities all having to do with the way your car's rear wheels line up with the front wheels. There obviously is a discrepancy. The cause is something else again.

To check, put the front wheels pointing directly ahead. Then, using a tape measure, check the distance from the center of the rear wheel to the center of the front on one side, then the other. I'm sure you'll find a difference.

The usual cause of this is an accident that causes damage to a car's structural integrity. That usually is quite difficult to fix.

Sometimes the rear spring shackles slip, allowing the car to shift in relation to the rear axle. This not only causes uneven wear patterns on the tires but makes the car appear to be moving "crabwise" down the road.

Chapter 13

Brakes

I have a 1972 Olds 88 Royale. I am getting a grab-grab-grab when braking and a rub-rub-rub when driving which increases in tempo as speed increases. I have had tires checked and wheels balanced and front-end alignment checked—all okay.

Various mechanics have road-tested the car and given such diagnoses as front disc rotors need cutting, left rear wheel bearing worn, left rear axle bent, right rear drum needs cutting, bad pinion in the rear, front tire out of round.

What do you think? Please advise before I go bankrupt.

This sounds like the multiple-guess tests we all had in school. Unfortunately, it also sounds like the last two answers in such an exam—all of the above or none of the above—could apply.

There are, however, a few things that could be done to at least eliminate some of the possibilities. For instance, the next time the car is in a garage for service, have the mechanic put it on a lift and run it in gear. If you have a bent axle, it will show up immediately as wheel wobble. In many cases, a worn axle bearing also will make noise when this test is done.

As for the discs needing cutting, if you pull the front wheels you'll be able to see very easily if there are deep scores that would require such action (Fig. 13-1). The same applies to the rear drums. With the car off the ground and the wheels off, this is plainly visible.

As for the front tire being out of round, that is easily enough tested on a dynamic wheel balancer that actually spins the wheel.

A bad pinion in the rear axle assembly would cause a very mild thumping noise, but should have no bearing whatsoever on the brakes—your grab-grab-grab.

If all of this checks out okay, I would check the condition of the brake system. Any number of problems could cause the brakes to fail to release or to release partially which would keep constant pressure on the disc rotors

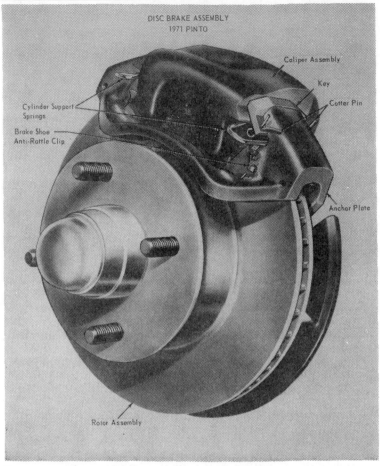

Caliper Assembly

Key

Cotter Pin

Cylinder Support
Springs

Brake Shoe
Anti-Rattle Clip

Anchor Plate

Rotor Assembly

Fig. 13-1. After removal of front wheels, the brake discs (or rotors) should look like this one. (Courtesy Ford Motor Company)

and rear drums. This would cause excessive heat which in time would warp your rotors, and this combination would result in both of the symptoms you describe. If this proves to be the case, be prepared to replace the rotors. If they are distorted by more than 10/1000 of an inch, they are as good as junk.

The brake pedal on my 1966 Thunderbird appears to be moving up and down as I apply pressure. The car is equipped with power disc brakes. What causes this and is it serious?

The symptom you describe is indicative of trouble, if not immediate, in the not too distant future. Most likely, it is caused by an imperfection on one or more of the brake discs. As pressure is applied and the brake lining binds against the disc, a vibration is set up that is transmitted back through the hydraulic system to your brake pedal. At the very least, it will cause unnecessarily fast wear of the linings. There also is a remote possibility that a brake assembly has worked itself loose and is setting up a vibration.

110

At 30,000 miles, I had new rear brakes put in and they have squealed ever since. I went back and they said nothing was wrong. They continue to squeal at 47,000 miles. The front brakes were put on earlier by a different man and they are all right. Please tell me what is the matter.

Your brake trouble is not so much a problem as an annoyance. Most likely, the man who relined your rear brakes used a harder composition lining than the original. This harder lining will last longer, but often results in squealing. It will not affect the car's stopping efficiency and, unless the noise is a real irritant, I would leave well enough alone. And, when the rears need relining the next time, have the work done by the same person who earlier did the fronts.

I have a Datsun 710 purchased new in December 1974. At 12,000 miles I had to have the front disc pads replaced and the rotors turned. It has just passed 20,000 miles and the same work has to be done again. I believe the caliper pistons are faulty, but a Datsun Service representative says that's not the case and there is nothing the company could do (under warranty). What recourse do I have?

I am inclined to agree that the caliper pistons are not the problem, although a malfunctioning relase valve in the master cylinder could cause the pistons to maintain higher pressure than normal, which would result in excessive pad wear.

Other possible problems are misalignment of the rotors—in relation to the wheel and/or axle—and incorrect compound of the pad. As for the rotor damage, this is being caused by using the brakes when the pads are worn out. The metal backing plate is scoring the rotor.

I have a 1968 Thunderbird with disc brakes. Can you tell me why the brake pedal seems to move up and down as I apply the brakes?

More than likely it is a result of a slight wobble in the brake discs. You should have them checked with a dial indicator and micrometer (Fig. 13-2). If there is more than a low degree disparity, the discs will have to be replaced (at a cost of about $80 each plus labor) or you run a serious risk of not having any brakes at all when you need them most.

We have a 1976 Chevette. Since we have no garage, the car is parked outside all night and when it rains, the car seems to have no brakes in the morning. When we do get the car to stop, it makes a grinding noise and pulls very hard to the left. Our dealer first told us there was nothing wrong, then promised to look into it. That was more than a month ago. Any suggestions?

It sounds very much like water is running down between the body panels—especially on the right front—and soaking the disc brake pad. This has the same effect as running through a large puddle of water in older drum-brake cars. In most applications, discs are not prone to this type of fade because the heat of the rotor quickly dissipates the moisture. But when it sits for several hours, the rotors cool and the pads get soaked.

As for the squeaking and pulling to the left, that is part of the drying out process. The left-side pad is drying out faster and providing more braking, thus pulling to the left.

To solve the problem, you should take the car to a Chevrolet dealer who has a water test stand. This is a device, most often used to find elusive leaks around windows and trunks, which pours copious amounts of water on a car—simulating a downpour. Immediately afterward, the mechanic should take it for a drive, which should reveal the problem.

I have a squeaky-noise problem with the power-assist disc brakes in my 1975 Dodge Charger SE. As a matter of fact, I had a similar problem with a '73. It seems to be just on the left front and started after about 2,000 miles. On the '73, they put something on the brakes but it didn't last more than a few hours. How can I get rid of that annoying noise every time I apply the brakes?

There are several silicone-based applications that are used in an attempt to rid disc brakes of squeaks and they work—as it did on your former car—for anywhere up to a month. For permanent relief, the only suggestion I can offer is to get a set of replacement pads with a softer compound lining. They won't last as long, but things should be considerably quieter.

My car is equipped with disc brakes, which are in need of replacement. Although I put linings on my earlier cars with drum brakes, I've never tackled the disc variety. Should I try it or am I better off taking it to the agency?

If you are experienced at relining drum brakes, you should have no trouble replacing the pads in your new car's disc brake system. In virtually all of the disc brake systems now in use on domestic and imported cars, relining disc brakes is considerably easier and faster (Fig. 13-3).

After jacking up the car—and supporting it with a jackstand, concrete block or other similar device—the wheel is removed. This will expose the disc brake system, which is composed of a rotor and caliper (some bigger luxury cars feature a dual caliper system).

The caliper contains two pistons that, when activated by the operator's pressure on the brake pedal, apply pinching pressure through the pads on the rotor. On the outward side of the caliper there are usually two fasteners—they can be thin bolts secured by nuts and lock washers or rods held in place by cotter pins or spring clips. To replace the pads, these fasteners must be removed and a screwdriver inserted from the side to keep the piston in a retracted position.

Depending on the placement of the caliper, the old pads either will fall out or be easily removed with a pair of needle-nosed pliers. While holding the piston back, drop the new pad in place. The same procedure should be repeated on the other side of the rotor before the retaining rods are reinserted.

Unlike your drum brakes, there is no need to adjust the new pads since discs are truly self-adjusting.

Incidentally, if your car is of domestic manufacture, the chances are very good that the rear brakes are of the old drum variety so don't give away those special tools just yet.

I have a 1972 Capri with a steering problem. It seems that when I go anything over 30 miles per hour and step on the brakes, the front end shakes uncontrollably. I have installed Koni struts, extra torsion bars and a hydraulic stabilizer. I also had the wheels aligned and dynamically balanced. I then replaced the brake pads. The problem still exists. Do you have any suggestions?

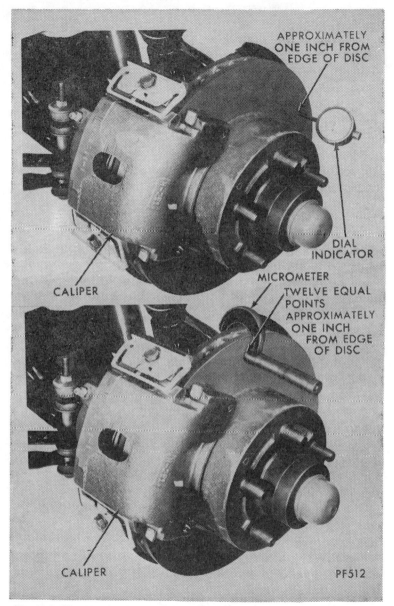

Fig. 13-2. Checking the condition of a disc brake rotor is accomplished with a dial indicator and a micrometer. (Courtesy Chrysler Corp.)

Assuming the tie rods and other pertinent pieces are in good shape, the problem is probably the brake discs themselves. If they are not turning on a level plane, or within 0.010 inch, you will get an adverse reaction when applying the brakes. Sometimes it shows up as a dangerously low pedal.

113

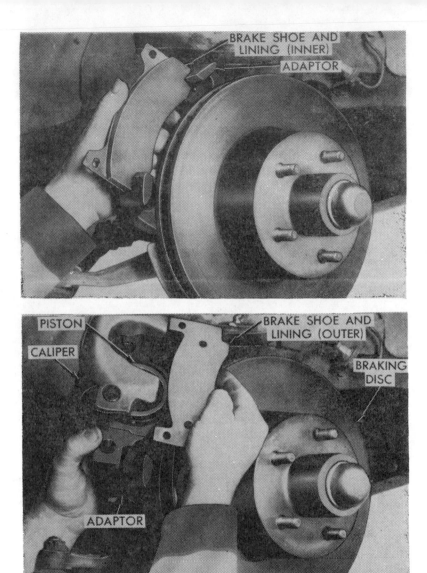

Fig. 13-3. After removing the retaining springs or clips, the caliper swings clear for simple installation of pads. (Courtesy Chrysler Corp.)

Other times it transmits a vibration back through the hydraulic system that results in an up-and-down motion of the pedal, even under steady pressure. And it often results in violent swerving of the kind you describe. I would take the car to a mechanic with a fine feeler gauge who can test whether your discs are out of line or not. If they are, the entire disc units will have to be replaced.

I have a 1973 Camaro with front disc and rear drum brakes, plus a proportioning valve between the front and rear systems. Since some sources recommend yearly replacement of the brake fluid with new, clean fluid, can you give me a backyard procedure for doing this? Also, will yearly replacement of the brake fluid system extend the life of the wheel cylinder and caliper parts between overhauls?

That's a new one on me. I have never heard it recommended that brake fluid be replaced every year.

However, if you are intent on doing the job, it is rather simple. Just open the bleeder valves on the back of each wheel and pump the brake pedal until nothing comes out. Then, after closing the bleeder valves, refill the system, pumping and bleeding each wheel by itself, and making sure always to have a sufficient amount of fluid in the master cylinder reservoir.

If the proportioning valve is operating properly, it will not interfere with this procedure.

I have a 1971 American Motors Ambassador that has a very hard brake pedal. I had new brake shoes and wheel cylinders installed but the problem persisted. It was almost as though there was no power assist and the car was difficult to stop.

The car then went to a dealer who replaced the drums, shoes, and cylinders. It didn't work. The master cylinder was changed and the power booster checked and declared to be working properly.

The car is dangerous to operate as is. Any ideas?

The usual cause for such problems lies with either the linings, shoes, or drums, but since all have been replaced, we'll have to look elsewhere.

Among the possibilities are clogged tubes or hoses which should be replaced; low vacuum supply to power brake booster which necessitates tuning or repairing engine to get adequate vacuum (14 inches minimum); loose or leaking hose to power-brake booster, requiring tightening or replacing hoses as needed; or faulty power-brake vacuum booster which calls for a new power section of the booster.

Any mechanic worth his grease should know of the test procedures for determining where the fault lies in your situation—it is not difficult and requires little more than a vacuum gauge in the way of tools. It appears the people you've been dealing with are more interested in selling parts than anything else.

Chapter 14
Tires and Wheels

I have a pair of studded snow tires showing very little wear. Since it will be unlawful to use such tires in New Jersey this year, would it be practical to remove the studs and use the tires as regular or snow tires?

Since more and more states are outlawing or have outlawed the use of studded tires, your dilemma is not unusual. The elimination of studded tires has come about because of the excessive damage they are causing to highway surfaces.

There is no reason in the world that you couldn't remove the studs and use the tires again. A word of caution, however; it is a long, hard, tedious job.

Those studs are put in there very firmly as is obvious by the fact that they stay in place at speeds well beyond the legal limit. If you pay to have them removed, I would estimate the cost at $10 per tire.

If you want to do it yourself, the best way is to use a pair of locking pliers and a heavy steel bar. Lock the pliers onto the end of the stud then, using the bar for a point of leverage, pry the stud out.

I have a Chevrolet. The booklet I got with the car recommends 24 pounds of air pressure in each tire. The attendants at the gasoline station always look at me in surprise when I say I want 24 pounds in the tires. They all say I should inflate the tires to 28 pounds, that at 24 the tires will wear much faster. At the lower pressure, my car rides much softer and quieter. What is your suggestion?

To quote the Tire Industry Safety Council: "Motorists may waste more than $100 million in needless tire wear this summer unless they pay more attention to proper inflation than usual." The biggest problem is caused by underinflation where the loss of 4 pounds of air pressure can reduce tread life by 10 percent and the loss of 12 pounds can cut it by 40 percent (Fig. 14-1).

116

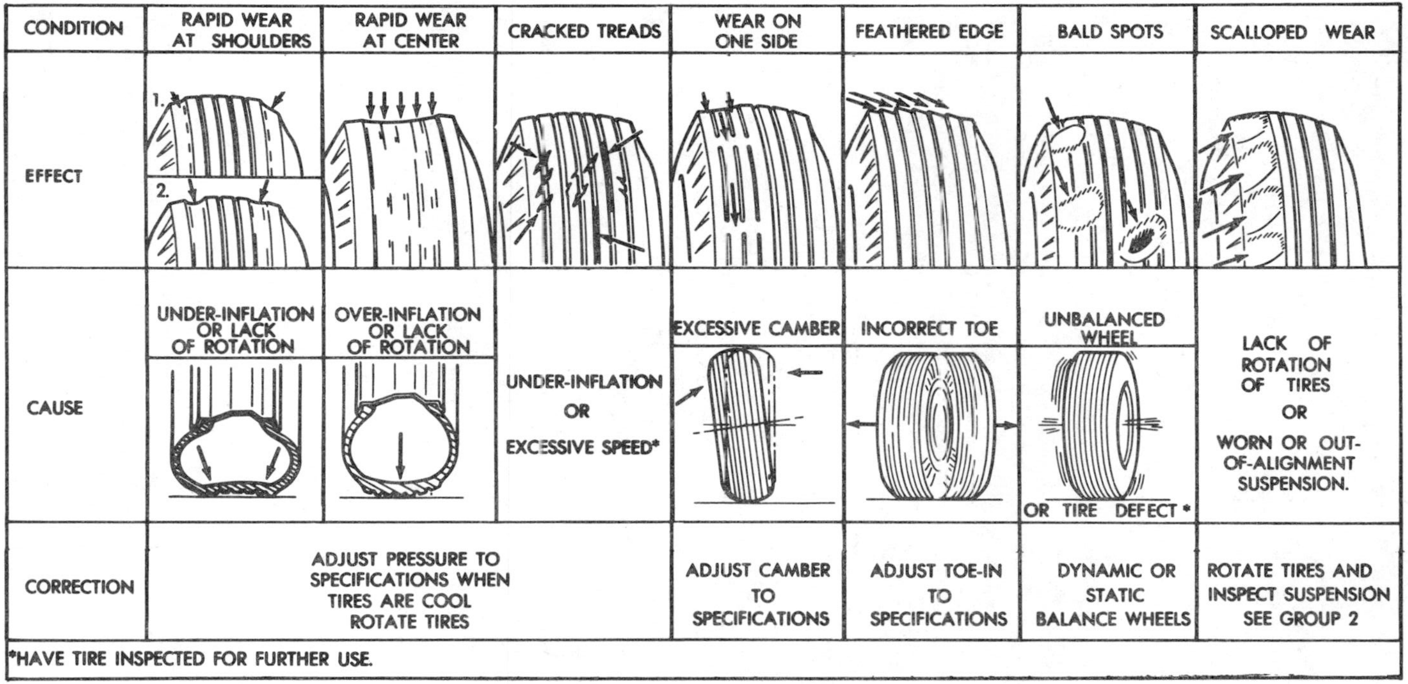

CONDITION	RAPID WEAR AT SHOULDERS	RAPID WEAR AT CENTER	CRACKED TREADS	WEAR ON ONE SIDE	FEATHERED EDGE	BALD SPOTS	SCALLOPED WEAR
EFFECT							
CAUSE	UNDER-INFLATION OR LACK OF ROTATION	OVER-INFLATION OR LACK OF ROTATION	UNDER-INFLATION OR EXCESSIVE SPEED*	EXCESSIVE CAMBER	INCORRECT TOE	UNBALANCED WHEEL — OR TIRE DEFECT *	LACK OF ROTATION OF TIRES OR WORN OR OUT-OF-ALIGNMENT SUSPENSION.
CORRECTION	ADJUST PRESSURE TO SPECIFICATIONS WHEN TIRES ARE COOL ROTATE TIRES			ADJUST CAMBER TO SPECIFICATIONS	ADJUST TOE-IN TO SPECIFICATIONS	DYNAMIC OR STATIC BALANCE WHEELS	ROTATE TIRES AND INSPECT SUSPENSION SEE GROUP 2

*HAVE TIRE INSPECTED FOR FURTHER USE.

Fig. 14-1. This illustration shows the effects and causes of under-inflation, over-inflation, and various other tire ills. (Courtesy Chrysler Corp.)

117

It seems to me that the manufacturer of your car knows considerably more about needed tire pressure—in relation to the weight of the vehicle and the size of the tires than any gas pump jockey. If the owner's manual recommends 24 pounds, I certainly would use 24 pounds.

There is one exception. If you are planning to do any sustained high-speed driving, it is advised that you add 4 extra pounds of pressure in each tire within the maximum allowable pressure that is indicated on the sidewalls.

Loss of tread life through overinflation is not as drastic as with underinflation, but it does occur. What happens is that the tire's footprint (the area touching the road surface) becomes rounded to the point where only the center portion is touching. This area then wears faster than it should.

Recently I bought a set of steel-belted radial tires along with a set of new shock absorbers. I have noticed that these new tires do not ride as smoothly as the old four-plies. I also have heard that they do not hold up on long trips at high speeds. One of my friends had two blowouts on the way to Florida. Is it true that the rubber does not adhere properly to the steel belts? Did I make the right move in buying these tires?

Although radial tires do have somewhat harsher ride characteristics than bias-ply tires, I think you more than likely are just noticing the difference from the rather soft ride you had previously. For example, the shock absorbers that you had on the car probably were pretty tired, giving you a softer (and more dangerous) ride than normal. Putting in new shocks firmed up the ride, and the addition of the radial tires accentuated the fact.

As for durability, a high-quality steel-belted radial will, in most instances, outperform a comparable bias-ply tire. I can only think that your friend got hold of a couple of bad tires because Goodyear and B.F. Goodrich, two of the largest tiremakers, have been involved in racing programs with their radials—subjecting street tires to much more speed, stress and, therefore, heat than any normal application could.

And, as for your making the right decision, I can only say that I would recommend radials over bias-plies in all applications where the car's suspension was tuned for radials at the factory—as virtually all now are.

When my 1965 Dodge Dart hits 50 miles per hour the front end vibrates violently. It will do this until it reaches 65 mph; then the ride is fairly smooth. What causes this?

Your problem could be caused by any number of front-end woes, including worn ball joints or tie rod ends, but the problem most likely is out-of-balance wheels (Fig. 14-1). I would recommend taking the car to any tire store and having the front wheels balanced. If this doesn't cure it, have the front end aligned. This would reveal any wear problems in other areas.

I have a 1968 Buick Special coupe with a 350-cubic inch V-8 engine, automatic transmission and power steering. The original tires that came with the car were 7.75/14. When I needed new tires, the salesman sold me F78/14. When I bought snow tires, they recommended 8.25/14. I would like to know if I can use H78/14 tires on the front or rear wheels because I get these tires for free.

With but few exceptions (Chevrolet's Monza 2-Plus-2 being one) the next size larger tire can be used in just about any application. In fact, many manufacturers recommend such a move when heavy-duty use of the vehicle is anticipated.

The F78s that you bought are the same as the 7.75s that were on the car in the first place. Federal regulations brought the lettering system into being because it is easier to understand. The 8.25 snowtires that you have correspond to G78, which are within the acceptable bounds.

I would not advise using the H78s on your car for two reasons. First, it is doubtful if your rims are wide enough to permit proper seating of the tire beads and this can be an unsafe situation. But, even were you to buy wider rims, there is a question of wheel well clearance and the distinct possibility of upsetting the suspension geometry.

In a recent column, you stated that radial tires should never be switched from side to side—only front to rear and vice versa.

The Owner's Manual for my 1973 Chrysler mentions both radials and other kinds of tires. It says that all tires should be rotated, using all five tires. The diagram given for the order of rotation shows side to side and/or diagonal rotation.

Has there been a change in proper rotation of radial tires since my Owner's Manual was printed, and how should I handle future tire rotation after already having used side to side or diagonal rotation?

I have received other similar letters questioning the same advice. According to several tire manufacturers, including Goodyear, radial tires develop a different wear pattern because of the increased tread flexibility provided by the radial construction. When you switch a radial tire to the other side of the car, this wear pattern is reversed and the tire will wear out much faster than it normally would.

Radial tire manufacturers recommend that in a five-tire rotation, the spare be placed on the right rear and the right rear be placed on the right front. The left rear should then go into the trunk as a spare. On the left side, the two tires should simply be switched (Fig. 14-2).

In bias-ply applications, where the wear pattern is less significant, the traditional rotation pattern should be followed. That includes spare to left front, left front to left rear, left rear to right front, right front to right rear and right rear to trunk.

Since the whole idea of this exercise is to keep radial tires rolling in the same direction—low-speed reverse applications notwithstanding—it probably would be feasible to cross over by dismounting the tires from the rims and remounting them in the opposite direction, but it hardly seems practical.

I have a 1972 Jeep Wagoner with standard H78/15 tires. The rims are 7 inches wide. I want to try steel-belted radial tires, with the primary objective being a softer ride. Would increasing the tire size make a proportionally softer ride and, if so, how far can I go without upsetting the overall operating relationship?

If your prime objective is a softer ride, you are looking in the wrong direction. There are many advantages to radials—they last longer and provide better adhesion, to name two—but they deliver a somewhat harsher ride than their bias-ply counterparts. As for using larger tires, the generally accepted rule is one size bigger, but no more. In your case that would be J78/15. However, I don't think this would noticeably increase the softness of your ride.

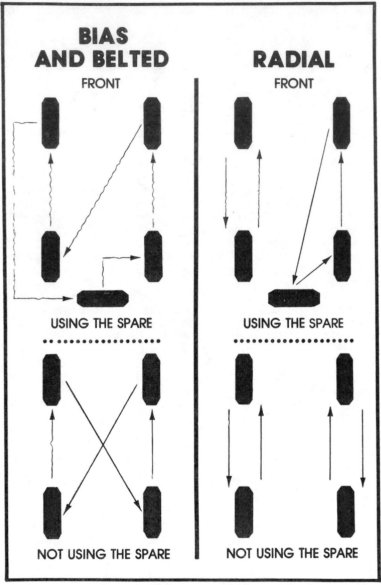

Fig. 14-2. This diagram shows the recommended four and five tire rotation for radial and bias-ply tires. (Courtesy B.F. Goodrich)

A note of warning: Many light-duty vehicles that were originally equipped with bias-ply tires do not have wheels of sufficient lateral strength to handle the stresses of radial tires. Under hard cornering, there have been cases of these wheels breaking or flexing enough to allow the tire's seal to break, with results similar to a blowout. If you still want to consider radials, I would check the suitability of your wheels with the manufacturer, not the tire salesman. Some unscrupulous people will agree to anything to make a sale.

We have a 1971 Ford Torino station wagon and soon will have to purchase four new tires. Typical of many station wagons, the ride is slightly unstable—it tends to fishtail. Could you recommend the type of tires to give the most stable ride—radials, belted or other?

For starters, I don't think that fishtailing is typical of the ride one can expect from a station wagon—unless you're driving it like it was a sports car. As for tires, radials generally give the best and longest service (at a higher initial price). But they are harsher riding and are not recommended for use on a car that did not come with them as original equipment—in many cases the wheels are not strong enough to stand the lateral stresses. I would look for a tire with the widest applicable footprint—probably "70" series belted. If nothing else, it will increase the surface rubber on the road.

I have read that regular snow tires should not be used in conjuction with radial tires on the front of a car. Why is this?

The Highway Users Federation for Safety and Mobility advises that it's both unsafe and unwise to mix bias-ply snow tires with radials because the driving characteristics of the two types are so different—mixing them can greatly increase your chances of slipping and skidding under wet conditions. What happens is that a radial tire (Fig. 14-3), which has a stiffer tread area and more flexible sidewalls, will grip the road better. Then, even though the front tires may retain traction (especially in turns), the bias-ply snows can break loose. This is something that might happen only 10 percent of the time when tires are mixed. But even 10-to-1 odds aren't very good when you're gambling on the possibility of losing control of a car.

I recently purchased a new car and, since I live in an area where winters are cold and snow is in abundance, I have sought and received a few opinions on snow tires.

The dealer from whom I bought the car says that with the radial tires I have, I shouldn't need snow tires. He has the same model car that I do and said he has never needed them himself.

I would like to know whether you think I should buy snow tires or try to get by on the regular radials.

A couple of years ago when General Motors made radial tires standard on many cars, it issued a statement to the effect that radials would prove a satisfactory substitute for snow tires in most applications.

This is an oversimplification. They do work even better than snow tires in light snow or ice conditons, but in a heavy, loose fall, they pack up very quickly and aren't much good. In your area, I would strongly recommend buying snow tires. Perhaps most importantly when you buy snow tires, make sure they are of radial construction. Due to adhesion factors, it can be extremely dangerous to mix radial and bias-ply tires on the same car.

I have read cautions about installing radial tires on older cars. What and how is the suspension tuned on the newer cars that are using radial tires?

Basically, it is in the way that the suspension systems are designed and built to handle loads. On cars built in "pre-radial" days, there was no need to build in protection against heavy lateral stress since the bias-ply tire would break loose (begin to slide) at that point.

With radials, the great flexibility of the tire's sidewall permits much greater traction during hard cornering, which means the suspension has to withstand this increased load.

There is a possibility, albeit remote, that an older suspension system could collapse in hard cornering applications, and that is why radials are not recommended for older cars.

Another problem is that the wheels built for bias-ply tires are not equipped for excessive lateral stress and also could break.

I have a 1975 Cadillac equipped with radial tires. I am not really sold on radials—they always look underinflated and I don't notice any appreciable difference in ride.

Would it be all right to go to a top-of-the-line belted polyester (or something similar) when replacement becomes necessary?

There is nothing in the book that says you can't use bias-ply tires on a car that was originally equipped with radials, although I personally would recommend staying with the latter.

Radials have several advantages over bias-ply tires in applications for which they are intended. Ride is not one. In fact, radials have a tendency to ride a little harsher and make a little more noise than the other type.

What radials do give you is longer life—as much as 50 percent or more—and, most importantly, better safety. A radial tire will have considerably more traction on both wet roads and in hard cornering because its more flexible sidewalls keep more of the tire's "footprint" on the road. This, incidentally, is why radials appear to be underinflated, which of course they are not.

I have a 1975 Honda CVCC. The manual calls for four snow tires. Would it be of any harm if I used two snow tires on the front (front-wheel drive) and my regular tires on the back?

Believe it or not, it is best in any application of snow tires to put them on all four wheels. But the manufacturers realize that the overwhelming majority of people can't understand the logic, so they don't harp on the subject.

The reason for this recommendation is that (in rear-drive application, which encompasses most cars), you can increase your steering capability in snow with foul-weather tires.

Using the same philosophy, it seems to me that you would be in an advantageous situation even if you only used snows on the front. It would increase your steering traction as well as driving traction. Four would be better, but two would suffice.

I have a 1971 Mercury Monterey and would like to know if I could use four belted tires in place of the four standard tires I now have (they are G78-15).

I have been told I can not use belted tires unless I make changes on suspension to accommodate the tires. Garages that sell tires say I need no suspension changes if I change all four tires. Mechanics say I need the change.

This is by far the grayest area for tire consumers. When you use the term belted tires, it is the vaguest possible because all tires are belted. Tires that most people consider standard are what the industry refers to as bias-belted, which means the belts of the tire are on the bias. Then there are

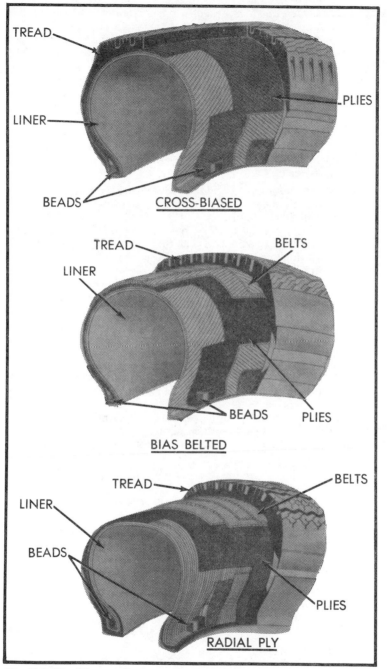

TREAD

LINER

BEADS CROSS-BIASED

PLIES

TREAD BELTS

LINER

BEADS PLIES

BIAS BELTED

TREAD BELTS

LINER

BEADS

PLIES

RADIAL PLY

Fig. 14-3. The differences in tire construction are readily visible in this series of cutaway drawings. (Courtesy Chrysler Corp.)

tires commonly referred to as belted, which also are on the bias, but are composed of different materials such as having some belts polyester and others fiberglass or some rayon and some steel. Then there are the radial tires in which the belts go around the circumference of the tire. They can be confused with the others because they are so often referred to as steel-belted radials, which most are.

As a rule of thumb, both tire and car manufacturers recommend that radial tires not be used on cars that weren't originally designed for radials, which is the case with your car. Because of a radial's inherently better traction, it can put more stress on the suspension than it was designed for.

As for "standard" and "belted" tires, since they are of the same basic construction, they are considered interchangeable on any car and are even suitable for use on cars designed for radials.

In a recent column you said that wheels built for bias-ply tires also are not equipped for excessive lateral stress and could break under extreme load conditions.

I recently purchased a 1977 Chevrolet Caprice and had snow tires mounted on new wheels. I was told by the tire man that the wheels were designed to match but he couldn't tell me how to identify that.

Would you tell me how I can tell whether the new wheels I purchased are the proper ones, those which would withstand the lateral stresses?

The information you were given is correct. There is no way to differentiate between wheels built for radial and bias-ply tires. Not to worry, however. Since virtually all cars built in the U.S. this decade have been built to use radial tires, so have all the wheels.

That which you refer to was in reference to using radial tires on older cars that were not designed for such use. Although some older wheels have been known to break under these conditions, the rate borders are being minuscule. That is because it only happens under extreme stress caused by very hard cornering. And the overwhelming majority of the people who drive a car that hard most likely would have high-performance wheels.

Chapter 15

Signs of Trouble:

Sights, Sounds, and Smells

The body of my 1968 Chevrolet has rusted through in several places. Otherwise, the car is excellent. It has only 49,000 miles on it and has never let me down. I have no desire to get rid of it, but the estimates I got from a couple of body shops are higher than I believe is reasonable to repair the holes, fix a couple of dents, and repaint the car. I have heard that there are fiberglass kits that can be used to repair auto bodies. Are these products as easy to use as the ads claim and do they really work?

They probably aren't as easy to use as the advertisement would have you believe. But what is? The fact is that if you follow the instructions carefully, you can get a virtually flawless repair job. The most important part of filling rust holes is to make sure you get the entire rust area clean. In many cases, you may begin to sand and find there is considerably more decay than you first thought. If you don't clean it all away, it'll just be a matter of time before the rust reappears.

If the holes are small—up to maybe 2 inches in diameter—the fiberglass repair kits do an excellent job.

After the area is prepared, alternating layers of the resin setting agent and the fiberglass sheets are applied (being sure to build up from a depth of at least ⅛-inch). It usually takes up to 24 hours to set, after which the area is sanded down to conform to the surrounding area.

The wood-grain paneling on the side of my station wagon seems to be turning cloudy or blotchy white. What causes this and how can I correct it? I've always taken excellent care of the car, having it washed regularly and waxed at least once a year.

Without knowing it, you answered your own question. The same thing is happening to the wood-grain siding (which is made of vinyl) that happens to all those kitchen floors you see in television advertisements—wax buildup compounded by water. You should obtain a wax-stripping product and give the siding a good going over. After than, an application of a vinyl cleaning agent should have it looking good as new.

For the past few years, I have noticed an increase in the number of small scratches on the windshield of my recreational vehicle. Can you tell me any way to get rid of them?

Rubbing the scratches with a cloth treated with any mild abrasive, such as toothpaste should have you seeing pretty in no time.

My daughter-in-law purchased a new Ford Pinto in 1972, and last year cracks started to appear on the (top of the) dashboard. They are getting wider every day. What could have caused this and can the Ford Motor Co. be held responsible?

It's generally caused by the extremes of heat and cold that the material goes through—especially when often exposed to extreme sunlight. Personally, I don't see how the company can be responsible since its warranty is only 12 months or 12,000 miles.

I have had a 1971 Volvo 142E for about two years. I recently opened the hood at night to investigate a noise and noticed that the exhaust manifold was so hot that it glowed in the dark. I don't know how long this has been happening or if it is out of the ordinary. I have checked with Volvo dealers about this but no one seems to know if anything is wrong. What do you think?

My man at Volvo tells me that it is perfectly normal for the exhaust manifold (Fig. 15-1) to give off a red glow at night. This is the spot where engine temperatures are at their hottest with the exception of the combustion chambers themselves.

I am concerned about what to do should my 1976 Buick start smoking under the floorboards because of the catalytic converter overheating. This car does not have a warning light to indicate such a problem. What can be done?

Although it is conceivable that the amount of heat generated by a converter could cause a smoldering fire, I have never heard of it happening to the car itself. I don't think you should concern yourself with this extremely remote possibility.

There are some precautions one should take, however. Never park the car in an area where there is flammable material, such as a field with dry grass or a garage that has papers or rags strewn about. There is enough heat to trigger a fire.

The warning light you mention is installed on some foreign cars. This is because at temperatures over the prescribed range, the catalyst in the converter will burn itself out and no longer remove the pollutants from the exhaust. It is not a sign of impending danger to the car or its occupants.

What would you check regarding the following? At 55 mph, my 1973 Pinto has a whining or humming noise and it's only at that speed. Through tests and examination, I have eliminated the engine, tires, and front wheel bearings. I have checked under the hood for possible looseness as well as the body for anything the air flow might be acting upon. Also had the speedometer pulled and lubricated. Any clues?

Although you had the tires checked, it is possible that this is where your noise is coming from. Depending on the composition, tread pattern and type

EXHAUST
MANIFOLD

Fig. 15-1. It is not particularly unusual for an engine's exhaust manifold to glow red at night, due to high temperatures. (Courtesy AMC)

of construction, some tires set up a humming noise that can be accentuated in a light car. Another possibility is the aerodynamic shape of your car. Sometimes a slightly different application of trim will set off wind noise at given speeds.

Can you tell me what a noise emanating from under the dashboard of a 1976 Chevrolet Impala might be? It sounds like an old electric clock shifting its movements. It seems to be less noticeable (or not at all) on warm days. Also, if this is in your line, I am holding on to my old car as its registration and inspection are good through July. I will only give up the old car if it fails to pass inspection. Is there any way to get the inspection without paying the registration fee and losing this money if it fails to pass?

It is possible that the under-dash noise is being caused by a faulty speedometer cable, but it's very possible that what you are hearing is the vacuum-operated heater-air conditioning switch. Anytime you move the control lever from off to heat or air condition, it is going to make a soft noise that is perfectly normal. If the noise is constant, it could be a minute leak in the vacuum line. As for your second car, the laws of your state require not only a valid registration slip, but a certificate of insurance of official state inspection. There is, however, an alternative. There are several service stations in your area that are licensed to certify the completion of repair work ordered by the state inspection stations and one of them might give your car a check to see if it would pass the official test.

Sometimes I hear a noise in my car, a 1974 Plymouth Duster with 6-cylinder engine. At about 30 miles per hour I hear what sounds like two pieces of metal clanging together but not too loud. Also, if I'm parked at a light and shift into a lower gear, I sometimes hear it. It also shows up sometimes going around a corner or up a hill.

Although it is very difficult to diagnose a noise without seeing the car, your problem sounds very much like something I went through with a 1951 Ford a couple of decades ago. Anytime I applied power (such as accelerating out of a corner or up a hill or, even revving it up in neutral), I got a noise similar to that you describe. It turned out to be a broken right-side engine mount (Fig. 15-2). Whenever power was applied, the natural tendency was for the torque to lift the right side of the engine. Eventually the left side mount broke, and the noise started coming whenever the brakes were applied (the engine actually slipped forward·and the fan clipped the radiator core). As a teenager, I didn't realize what was happening until the fan had chewed deeply enough into the radiator to cause a leak that couldn't be repaired—a most-expensive lesson. I would advise checking both the radiator core and shroud for tell-tale signs of such a problem.

When I was out-of-state for an extended period, my luxury car was stored in a closed garage and developed an aggravated case of mildew on its leather seats (and elsewhere). Surfaces were wiped clean with a commercial disinfectant and the car aired outside for weeks with windows open to dry the damp interior, but the strong odor characteristic of mildew persists. Any suggestions?

I have both bad news and good news for you. The bad news is that your car has developed a problem for which there is no permanent cure. The good news is that with proper attention on a schedule of about once a year it can be kept under control.

Unlike germs, which can be eradicated with the use of a good commercial deodorant, mildew is a fungus that is not affected by those products. Instead, make your own mixture in this manner: Combine 3 quarts of water with 1 quart of laundry bleach, an ounce of laundry detergent and 3 ounces of trisodium phosphate (available in hardware stores).

Using a sponge, apply the solution to all readily accessible interior surfaces. At the same time, try to squeeze a fair amount of the liquid into joints and crevices where colonies often survive. And while you're at it, it wouldn't hurt to give the trunk a good wipedown, too.

I have a 1976 Plymouth Volare Custom coupe with a six-cylinder engine, automatic transmission, and power disc brakes. It has an annoying whistle in the motor when I accelerate. I have asked several dealers about this and have received no satisfactory reason for the whistle. I am hoping you can advise me of the cause and what I might be able to do about it.

I am inclined to think that the noise you hear is simply caused by the rush of air through the air cleaner as your acceleration calls for it, although it could be a malfunction of the air cleaner case.

The first thing I would do is to completely remove the air cleaner and give it a close visual check to make sure there are no cracks or bad seals in the case or the gasket that fits between the air cleaner and the top of the carburetor.

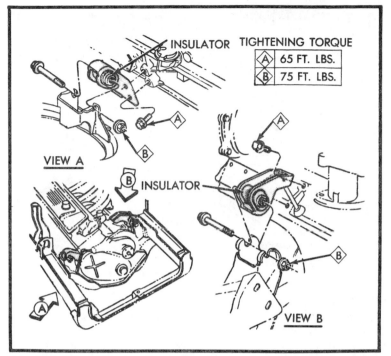

Fig. 15-2. This is the way the front motor mounts for the 225 six-cylinder Plymouth engine function. (Courtesy Chrysler Corp.)

If this checks out, make sure the filter element is in good shape—that it is clean enough to do the job and that it is in no way distorted. To check the cleanliness, hold it up to a strong light. You should be able to see some light.

Put everything back together the way it came apart. If you still get the noise, try repositioning the air inlet horn—move it toward a more frontal position.

Another possibility, although I consider it remote, is that a pinhole leak has developed in the gasket between the carburetor and intake manifold. I say remote because such a leak would cause a constant noise that would grow louder on acceleration.

About a year ago, I purchased a middle-priced convertible top from Sears for my wife's 1968 Firebird. Probably due to being kept outside all the time, the plastic window surface has become badly pitted and, at the bottom, it is very frosted. We have always cleaned it as directed, but visibility is getting worse.

Is there any way to restore some of the visibility, or must I put in a new window? And, if I need a new window, how do I go about it?

The first thing I would try, is cleaning the window with the mildest abrasive you can find—toothpaste often will do the job.

If, however, you are unable to get satisfactory results, I would advise replacing the entire window assembly. Assuming you installed the top yourself, you are familiar with the steps necessary to remove the plastic window and surrounding canvas and half the zipper.

Despite the fact that nobody's making convertibles anymore, there are still shops that specialize in replacement tops. You should take the piece and have them sew in a new window—it shouldn't cost you $25.

Then, replace the window assembly taking care to zip it back to the top first. If you attach it to the bottom first, you stand a very good chance of a loose fit, at best, or one so tight you won't be able to zip it.

The fuel gauge on my 1976 Pacer registers empty most of the time. Because of this problem, I keep the tank continually full. In spite of three trips to the dealer, their efforts to repair it do not last long. What could be the matter?

I am inclined to think it is probably a loose electrical connection or a broken wire somewhere between the sender unit in the fuel tank and the dashboard gauge (Fig. 15-3). The reason I think this is because you indicate that the problem is intermittent. A loose connection could cause the assembly to work sporadically. So could a broken wire that occasionally touches what it isn't supposed to.

If that isn't it, I would do an electrical continuity test on the sender unit itself—it is located on the outside of the tank. As a last resort, I would check the dashboard gauge.

When I start my 1973 Chevrolet Impala, I get a screeching sound. It usually stops in a few seconds. Other times, I have to drive awhile before it subsides.

It seems that I only get this sound on cold days after the car has been standing. Is there any way I can have it corrected?

There are several possibilities, most likely of which is a loose fan belt. When the belt is loose and you start a cold engine, the somewhat more brittle belt scrapes across the various pulley surfaces and produces a screeching noise.

It is a simple condition to diagnose. With the engine off, reach down and press on the fan belt. If it moves more than half an inch, it is too loose and should be tightened by loosening the adjusting bolt on the alternator and moving the alternator farther away from the engine block. Then retighten the bolt and check again.

Take care not to get it too tight, however, because that condition will put excess strain on both the water pump and alternator bearings, and it won't be long before you have a similar noise. And that is where the other possibilities lie. If the belt proves to have the proper tension or is too tight, there is a distinct possibility that either the water pump bearing or alternator bearing is failing. Your mechanic can check those possibilities in a matter of minutes.

My wife and I are planning a motor trip to Los Angeles during the month of July in our 1976 Buick Skylark, which now has 2,100 miles on it. Since we see this as a chance to relax and see the country, we would not rush or speed to save time. The car has a V-6 engine, air conditioning, automatic transmission, power steering, power brakes, and steel-belted radial tires. The car is reasonably quiet and comfortable, and we have experienced no maintenance problems as yet.

Would you please comment on what we might expect in the way of maintenance problems, comfort, economy, and car equipment that we should pack before we leave. An ounce of prevention is still worth more than a pound of cure.

I think that most of the standard rules of highway travel apply in your case. Even though you may have by no means reached the recommended mileage of service, I would have the car lubricated and the oil and filter changed before leaving. At that time, have the mechanic give the car a check—fluid levels in battery, transmission, power steering, radiator, and tires. At the same time, he might check the alignment—it's been a rough winter for potholes.

If you're at all mechanically inclined, take along a small tool kit consisting at least of a large and small screwdriver, a Phillips head screwdriver, standard pliers, slip-joint pliers, and an adjustable wrench.

We have a new Volkswagen Rabbit which has a very loud vibration, particularly in deceleration, coming from the exhaust system pipes. A local VW repairman says it is caused by vibration of these pipes, up to a couple of inches, and could be fixed by welding some brackets to steady the pipes.

However, he's reluctant to do this because it might break the rust-proofing seal and could jeopardize the guarantee. Our VW dealer, who has been consistently bad in the service area, says he doesn't have to fix the problem under warranty because there is no actual flaw in the "original equipment."

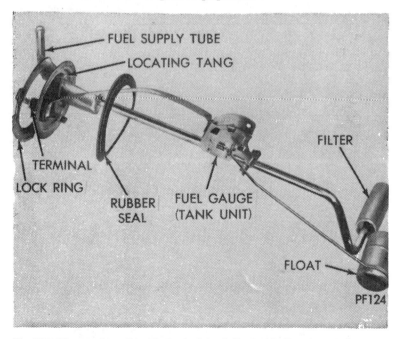

Fig. 15-3. The sender unit inside the tank is similar to this Chrysler unit. It's not complicated, but every part is critical. (Courtesy Chrysler Corp.)

I think the dealer should take the responsibility for this. What should we do?

There is no doubt in my mind that the problem should be fixed by the dealer under warranty. It seems that more and more dealers are simply interested in selling cars and doing repair work upon which they can make a good profit.

Volkswagen, which had one of the best dealer network reputations in the industry just a few years ago, seems to be losing control. This, of course, isn't restricted to VW. Many others are having the same problem.

I would insist that the dealer make the needed repairs and, if that doesn't work, I would write to Volkswagen of America in Englewood Cliffs, N.J., giving them complete details.

Should this also fail, which is not beyond the realm of possibility, I would have your independent repairman weld on the required brackets. He can apply a high-temperature paint—known generically as manifold paint—to the welds to protect against rust.

Chapter 16
Potpourri: Problems, Problems

In one of your earlier replies you referred to roll bars being installed in convertibles. I have a 1966 Cadillac convertible. Where could I have this installation done, preferably as close to home as possible?

Any store that specializes in high performance automobile accessories should be able to provide the information you seek. The best bet, however, is to have the bar installed by a reputable machine shop,using steel tubing of the proper composition and size to actually support your car in event of a flip. Since your car is so big and heavy, it quite possibly might not be feasible.

Can you explain why the automakers no longer offer vent windows in the front doors of today's cars? I always found them very nice, and I would be willing to pay extra if I could buy a car that offers them.

It's strictly a matter of cost. The average manufacturer's saving for vent windows is about $100 per car, a savings that the automakers presumably pass on to the consumers in a slightly lower sticker price. You might ask then why they don't offer the vent windows as a $100 option. The answer is that to tool up for two different types of windows on each model of car would drive the cost well over that $100 figure. There are some current cars that do offer vent windows as standard features. Among them are the pull-open type on the AMC Pacer, the crank type of Audis, and the power window of the Lincoln Continental.

Has there ever been any suggestion as to how a passenger can stop a car when the driver becomes ill or otherwise incapacitated. With power steering and power brakes, you couldn't very well turn off the ignition. Any suggestions?

You are quite correct in assuming that shutting off the ignition might cause more problems than it would solve. Were something like this to happen to me, I would move the shift lever into neutral, take control of the steering wheel, and use my left foot to slow the car with the brake pedal. Moving the lever into neutral is a very simple procedure on virtually every car as long as you apply both forward and upward pressure. There is a built-in shoulder in the mechanism that prevents the lever from going into reverse unless the lever is pulled toward the operator while moving it upward. Should such a crisis develop on a car with standard shift, you should again put it in neutral (it might take a little more effort to force it out of gear) and then go for the brakes. Whatever, do not panic. Almost always, a sick driver is preferable to a panicky passenger.

I recently purchased a 1967 Chevrolet Corvair, ignorant of the fact that serious driving problems may exist. What exactly prompted a stoppage of Corvair production, and do I have a safety problem that I should be concerned with?

Chevrolet introduced the air-cooled, rear-engine Corvair compact in 1960 in an attempt to counter the growth of foreign car sales in the United States. In the first few years of production, there were suspension problems that, in some cases, led to rollovers that—experts testified—probably would not have happened in cars with more conventional suspensions.

Chevy engineers corrected this problem in the 1964 model and there were no such problems after that.

Production was stopped in the late 1960s simply because the demand for the car had dropped by about 90 percent—due largely to the adverse publicity it received.

Assuming that your 1967 is in good operating condition—shocks, springs, bushings and linkage all functioning properly—you should have no problems along these lines in normal driving. If you have a penchant for driving it like a sports car, feel it out first because a rear-engine car has different characteristics from those of a front-engine car.

And, as a bonus, Corvairs of that vintage in good condition are appreciating in value as fast or faster than most recent-model cars.

Several months ago, I bought a new Mercury Monarch Ghia and I've taken it back to the dealer four times in an attempt to eliminate a problem of water building up inside the trunk when it rains. The dealer can't seem to find the trouble. Any suggestions?

If the car has been back to the dealer four times, I presume they have checked and rechecked the rubber molding around the inside of the trunk lid where most leaks of this type originate. The only other area that might cause trouble like this is around the rear window itself. If the rubber molding is not perfectly fitted to both the glass and surrounding body, water can leak into the trunk—sometimes in great amounts. I would suggest running a hose on this area while checking inside (Fig. 16-1). If it shows this is where the leak is you might be able to cure it by a liberal application of silicone sealant, several brands of which are available.

If the leak is in that area and the sealant doesn't stop it, chances are it will require removal of the window and refitting new molding, a new window or both. But with the car less than a year old, it should be covered under warranty.

I am seeking advice on how I can best make my 1972 Gran Torino station wagon last as long as possible. It has 107,000 miles on it and I have been careful about getting it in for servicing at the

proper time. **Can you advise me about what particular problems I should be aware of and at what point I should give up on keeping the car?**

In these days of soaring prices, both for new cars and the parts and service to keep old ones running, this is a problem that has many Americans in a quandary. It also is not an easy question to answer because there are so many variables. For instance, if the body, paint and interior are in reasonably good condition, the car most likely would be worth enough to warrant the investment of several hundred dollars in repairs should the need arise. On the other hand, if the car looks like it has 107,000 miles on it, chances are you would be throwing good money down the drain by having major repairs done to it. I have often said—and fervently repeat—that there is no reason that a car can not be expected to deliver 100,000 miles of service if it is given reasonable care. From the sound of it, I would say your wagon has been serviced regularly. However, once you pass 100,000 miles, you are on borrowed time. There are thousands of parts that go into the construction of a car and, at high mileage, any can go bad. My advice is to keep on as you have. Get the car serviced at regular intervals and don't hesitate about having minor repairs done. But, if something major goes wrong, such as transmission failure or internal engine problems, think twice before having the work done.

I would like to tow my 1973 Oldsmobile Delta 88 with automatic transmission and power steering across the country. I would tow with my ¾-ton pickup truck. My concern is, can I tow a vehicle that has a locking steering wheel? The ignition switch locks the steering. If it is possible, what preparations should I make?

For starters, I would not recommend towing at speeds above 35 miles per hour, for obvious safety reasons. As for your locking steering wheel,

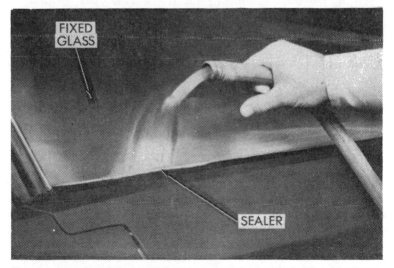

Fig. 16-1. If the trunk lid seal is tight, check around the rear window with a liberal dosing of water. Sealant works here. (Courtesy Chrysler Corp.)

why not just use the key to turn it on? If you are worried about running down the battery because the ignition is on, that can be handled simply by disconnecting the battery's ground wire because that will avoid sparks that could, under the right circumstances, trigger a battery explosion. I'd also disassemble the rear universal joint to eliminate potential transmission damage.

Don't forget to rig a safety chain between the vehicles and to hookup wiring so you'll have taillights and brake lights on the towed vehicle.

A friend has offered to sell me his pop-up camper at what I believe to be a very good price. He said I will be able to tow the trailer without a lot of unnecessary trailer goodies. What is your opinion?

It depends on what he is calling unnecessary trailer goodies. What you will need is a Class One hitch for your car, four-way plug with which to hook up your car's turn signals, taillights, and brake lights to the trailer, an emergency chain, and at least one removable mirror for the right side. If he is referring to such items as transmission oil cooler, heavy-duty suspension pieces, and the like, he is correct. From a towing point of view, a pop-up camper is the most efficient way to go.

I'd like your opinion of the miles-per-gallon gauges on the market and the claim that they can help one drive more economically.

If you drive by them, they can save you gas. Detroit, however, found that most people were annoyed by the flashing lights and swinging dial indicators.

The whole secret to economical driving is to maintain a light touch, especially on acceleration.

We recently bought a 1971 Opel station wagon only to discover that it needs a new carburetor. It has been very frustrating trying to find a place that sells parts for this car. I need the car for work. Do you have any suggestions?

All of the questions I get should be this simple to solve. Any Buick dealer should be able to supply you not only with the needed carburetor, but with any other part you might need for your Opel. That's because the German Opel is a wholly owned General Motors subsidiary and was sold in the United States by Buick dealers as what the industry terms a captive import.

Would you be so kind as to help me settle a friendly argument? Does a car rust more quickly during the winter if it is parked inside a garage or left outside in the snow? We live in the snow-belt region and salt is used on the roads throughout the winter season.

The best way to minimize rust damage in areas where the roads are constantly and heavily salted is to park the car in a heated garage so that any accumulation of salt-laden snow and ice can melt away and then flood the inner fender wells with a hose to wash away any residue. If you don't wash it away, the salt buildup eventually will cause decay. If the temperature in your area is, for the most part, below freezing you would have less damage if you let the car remain in the cold than if it melts without being flushed. Rust problems, however, are becoming less and less a factor as time goes on. In addition to improved undercoating techniques, most autobuilders are using zinc-coated steel in areas that have been particularly prone to rust (Fig. 16-2).

My 16-year-old son wants to put chrome outside exhaust pipes on the family car. My mechanic says it's illegal even though there are cars and vans running around that way. Exactly what is the law about those pipes?

Your mechanic is right. In Pennsylvania and many other states, it is illegal to change a vehicle's exhaust system from the stock factory configuration. If you want to install dummy pipes for show purposes only that is permissible. The vehicles you see with such pipes probably had them new as factory options.

I have two Motor's Auto Repair Manuals and would like some idea of what they are worth. One gives instructions on the removal, replacement, fitting, and adjustment of all mechanical parts on all cars built from 1935 to 1948. The other manual covers cars built betwen 1940 and 1954.

Like the cars that are covered in the manuals, they themselves are valuable only to a limited special interest group. If you come across somebody with a 1938 Willys or whatever who likes to do his own tinkering, the book would have some value. But, since Motor and its prime competitor, Chilton, still offer new versions of these old books for less than $20, I wouldn't set my sights too high.

My car has an oil bath air filter with the cleaner in the top half of it. What type of cleaner should I use for the air filter and how often should I clean it? The last cleaning was at 97,000 miles and the car now has almost 99,000. I have owned the car several months now and I am not yet familiar with the oil bath feature of my 1954 model car.

The frequency needed in cleaning your air filter depends, of course, on the type of driving you do. If you operate the car in areas where there is considerable dust and dirt in the air, you should clean it about once every 1,000 miles or so. Under more normal conditions, it can be done at intervals of as much as 3,000 miles.

Cleaning the unit is a fairly simple, but dirty job. After taking care to keep it level as you remove it from the carburetor, pour the oil into an appropriate container—a used milk carton is adequate. Then wipe the remaining oil from the inside surface and take a clean rag soaked in gasoline to complete the clean up—including the wire mesh area.

Refill with fresh oil to the level indicated by a stamping on the side. It should be 20 or 30 weight and can be the cheapest you can find—even re-refined or remanufactured.

In September, I purchased a 1976 Chevette with a 1.6-liter engine, automatic transmission, and air conditioning. The EPA mileage rating for this car is 29 miles per gallon for combined city-highway driving.

I am very disappointed to find that I average between 18 and 19 miles per gallon. I have brought the car back to the dealer twice, and all they do is make adjustments according to factory specifications. They say the mileage will improve as the engine is broken in, but after 2,000 miles, I notice no improvement.

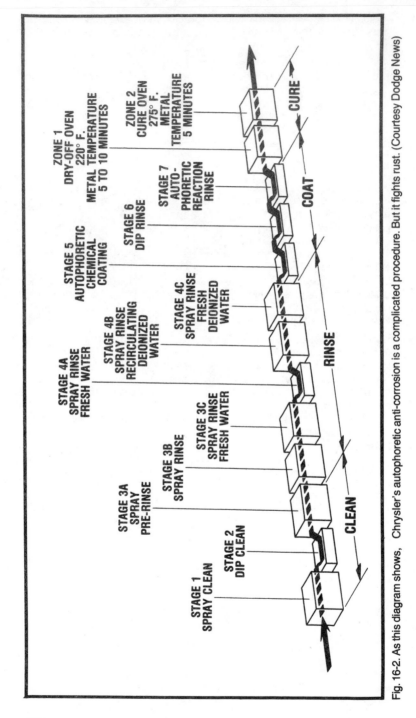

STAGE 1
SPRAY CLEAN

STAGE 2
DIP CLEAN

STAGE 3A
SPRAY
PRE-RINSE

STAGE 3B
SPRAY RINSE

STAGE 3C
SPRAY RINSE
FRESH WATER

STAGE 4A
SPRAY RINSE
FRESH WATER

STAGE 4B
SPRAY RINSE
RECIRCULATING
DEIONIZED
WATER

STAGE 4C
SPRAY RINSE
FRESH
DEIONIZED
WATER

STAGE 5
AUTOPHORETIC
CHEMICAL
COATING

STAGE 6
DIP RINSE

STAGE 7
AUTO-
PHORETIC
REACTION
RINSE

ZONE 1
DRY-OFF OVEN
220° F.
METAL TEMPERATURE
5 TO 10 MINUTES

ZONE 2
CURE OVEN
275° F.
METAL
TEMPERATURE
5 MINUTES

CLEAN

RINSE

COAT

CURE

Fig. 16-2. As this diagram shows,   Chrysler's autophoretic anti-corrosion is a complicated procedure. But it fights rust. (Courtesy Dodge News)

I understand that the EPA ratings are higher than one actually gets, but should we expect only 66 percent of those estimates? Please note that the 19 mpg average was attained without using the air conditioner. Any suggestions?

First off, the fact that you realize the EPA is a perennial optimist when it comes to auto mileage figures puts you ahead of most people. I have found as a general rule that the EPA figures are between 10 and 20 percent on the high side. Taking the high percentage (or 6 miles per gallon), 23 would be a more realistic figure.

Another thing that you—and most American drivers—do not realize is that the weight of the air conditioning unit is considerable, and it will deduct from your mileage whether you actually use it or not. It becomes even more of a factor in a little car since it adds a bigger percentage of weight.

This, combined with the fact that the EPA tests are done on cars equipped only with *standard* equipment, can drop the legitimate estimate as much as 2 to 3 miles per gallon. And that brings the figure close to what you are getting.

All U.S. automakers have discontinued convertibles. I have read that the reason is that no one buys them. I also have read that it is due to new federal safety standards. Is either reason valid and, if so, how do the foreign makers continue to sell convertibles here?

Both reasons are right as far as the U.S. manufacturers are concerned. Over the last decade, sales of American-built ragtops have dropped more than 90 percent to less than 100,000 units in the 1975 model year. American Motors, the smallest of the Big Four, was the first to eliminate convertibles in the late 1960s.

There are National Highway Traffic Safety Administration regulations that accelerated the trend. There is a rather complicated formula that takes into consideration such things as the roll-over factor, engine horsepower, total weight of the car, and its center of gravity, according to a spokesman for British-Leyland which, with its MGs and Triumphs, is now the leading producer of convertibles for the American market. Both MG and Triumph are relatively lightweight, low-powered cars with a low center of gravity and minimal roll-over factor. They therefore do not need built-in rollbars although more and more owners are having them installed.

I have a 1974 Dodge Dart which has leaked over the driver's leg area ever since I got it. It seems to be right above an open area where wires come through (the firewall) over the hand brake. I am afraid to go out when it rains hard, as I am sure to get water on my legs, not to mention the car's carpet. My dealer put cement around the windshield and I tried some silicone sealer, but it still leaks. What can be done to stop the leakage?

The water is leaking in through one of three places—around the windshield, through the fresh air vent, or through that firewall hole, which should not be open the way you describe it. Since the windshield has received attention more than once (all the way around I presume), I would bet on the fresh air vent. To check it, flood the area with water from a hose (Fig. 16-3) and check underneath to see where it's coming from. That will enable you to give your service manager a better idea of the problem. That hole in the firewall isn't so much a potential leak area as it is a hazard from fumes in the engine compartment. There is a substance that body men call dum-dum which is available in most auto supply stores. It is a pliable material that can be spread over this area to seal it.

How can somebody who is inexperienced at dealing with repair shops or automobile agencies avoid being taken?

Recently my windshield wiper stopped working. I went to a dealership repair shop where, two hours later, the car was ready and I received a bill for $30.98. The only part on the bill was a windshield relay at $6.80.

I have had a nagging feeling that I have been had. Could you tell me if I could have approached the problem in a different way? And what is a good approach when taking a car in for repair so a person is not taken for a dummy?

The term "windshield relay" leaves me at a loss. I can only surmise that it has to do with an intermittent wash/wipe system which would have to be regulated by a relay-type unit. At any rate, most of the expense involving automobiles lies in the labor required to make the repairs, rather than the cost of the replacement parts.

As to this specific instance, I would not say that you were ripped off. At the very least, the mechanic had to work from a prone position under the dashboard. Or, he had to remove cowling to get at the piece.

As to an approach for taking a car in for repair work, or for routine service, a virtual art form has developed. The idea is not to appear like you know what's going on unless you really do.

When it comes to dealing with auto service people, a little knowledge can be worse than none. So many times a person will take his not-quite-perfectly running car for service and tell the mechanic something like, "It isn't running right. Would you give it a tune-up?" Well, the mechanic or the

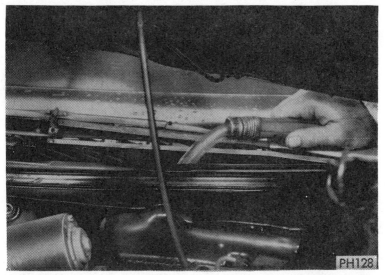

Fig. 16-3. To check for possible leak in fresh-air vent, run water through grillework at rear of hood, then check under dash area. (Courtesy Chrysler Corp.)

service writer, is in business to make a profit. His primary enterprise is selling parts and labor. If you ask for a tune-up, that's what you're going to get, even if you don't need it.

The simple fact is that you very well might need only adjustment of the ignition timing or the carburetor. But what you'll get are new breaker points, spark plugs, and all the rest that goes with a tune-up, at a cost considerably higher than you should have spent.

Let's face it. If you ask for something, a good business person is going to give it to you. And that should not be construed as being dishonest. A little shady maybe, but not dishonest.

The best way to handle the situation is to get yourself some working knowledge of the car—an adult education course is the best way, but even a thorough reading of the owner's manual is a help. That will help put you on the same wavelength with the vehicle. You should be able to understand a little of what the different sounds and feels are. Armed with this, you can give a mechanic some idea of what is (or isn't) going on.

The idea when you go in for repairs is to describe, as accurately as possible, the symptoms. But don't say something like "The transmission is acting up." An unethical person might sock you $250 for an overhaul when all you really need is a band adjustment for about $30.

Things like that happen more often than one might imagine. And the primary reason is that most people seem to be ashamed to admit that they don't know it all.

Believe me when I say that most mechanics don't know it all. Like other professionals, the auto repair business is a haven for specialists. A person who is very proficient at doing tune-up work might not know beans about automatic transmissions and vice versa.

If you think something is wrong and can give the mechanic an accurate description of what it feels or sounds like, the chances are very good that it can be fixed at the cheapest possible price.

But you can't expect to always get away for a few dollars. Not only is the mechanic out to make a living, but chances are he has considerable overhead to pay for. As cars get more and more complicated, it takes an increasing amount of diagnostic equipment to be able to repair them efficiently. We, the motoring public, must pay for those things. And a big shop will charge more than a one-man operation for labor because the pie must be divided more ways.

I recently have been widowed and own a 1976 Dodge Sportsman Royal van. Since I am now responsible for the upkeep, could you advise me on a class that would give me the general things a woman should know or could do rather than take the van to a garage too frequently?

In recent weeks, the brakes went out and a new cylinder had to be installed. Then, something went wrong with the rear axle and I had to have it fixed. It was still in the warranty period so it cost me nothing. I would appreciate any advice you could give me.

From the tone of your letter, I get the impression that you would like to learn auto mechanics on a rather grand scale. If that is your intention, I advise you to forget it. There is simply too much involved.

However, there are courses available, usually at a local community college (or its equivalent) and at the adult school division at area high schools, that can teach you some very valuable basics. Generally, these courses give you a working background on the motor car. They tell you, in layman's terms, how an automobile functions. They help you recognize sights, sounds, and smells that can indicate problems. Additionally, most of them will teach you how to do basic repair and maintenance items such as lubrication, oil change, replacing points and plugs, and so forth. Small jobs that you can do at a considerable saving.

The problems that you have experienced probably would be too complicated for you to attempt to fix yourself which, of course, you wouldn't attempt in the warranty period.

The best advice I can give anyone in such a situation is to take a basic auto maintenance course—but only if he or she has a real interest in the subject and some mechanical aptitude.

Then be sure that your car, truck, van or whatever gets the required service when it is due. If a vehicle is serviced regularly by competent technicians, there's no reason you can't expect to get 100,000 miles out of it.

Remember, you must pay for service sooner or later. The questions are when and how much. If you let it go, you'll undoubtedly wind up paying a lot more later for major service that could have been avoided.

I have a 1968 Buick Skylark coupe with about 50,000 miles on it. After a small accident, the car was idle for several months. When it wouldn't start, I had a mechanic look at it and he replaced the following items: engine oil, filter, transmission fluid, coil, distributor cap, rotor, plugs, points, condenser, plug wires, battery cables, exhaust system, headlights, antifreeze, air and gas filters, brake fluid, and others. After all this, it still wouldn't start and a second mechanic said the car still needs a major tune-up that would cost $150 to $200. Could you please tell me what the car needs and is it worth another $150 for a major tune-up, whatever that is?

It sounds like the first guy saw you coming and pounced on you like a vulture. And the second guy really wants to get in on the action. Many of the things you mentioned should be changed after a car with 50,000 miles on it sits idle for an extended period of time. That includes oil, filters, antifreeze, and the transmission fluid. The rest of it sounds like the guy started at one point and worked his way around hoping to strike upon the faulty piece. And all at your expense.

Unfortunately, I have no way of knowing exactly what your car's problem is without at least looking at it. But there are several areas that you do not mention that might be the cause. One is the carburetor. By pouring raw gas through it, you might be flooding the engine. Another is the fuel pump. If it's bad the engine won't be getting enough fuel, if any. Yet another is the ignition timing. If it's off, the engine can not start. And, how about the battery? If it's old enough and tired enough, it might have enough juice to crank the engine but not enough to provide a good, strong spark.

My advice is to find a mechanic you can trust (ask friends and neighbors just as you would in looking for a doctor or a dentist). The shop should have sufficient diagnostic equipment so that the mechanic shouldn't have to resort to the old trial-and-error method as the first guy did. There is no way that it should cost $150 or $200 for a major tune-up, which includes much of what you have already had done plus timing, carburetor adjustment, and other

142

diagnostic work. Major automotive outlets usually get up to $50 or so for such work.

I wish you luck.

I purchased a new Pinto Pony last April. After about 10 weeks and 1,800 miles, the fuel gauge stopped working. When the tank is filled, it moves to full and the needle will not move until after eight or nine gallons are used. Then it moves, barely to the first marker.

I have taken the car back to the dealer seven times. Each time the mechanics have done all they could think of, including a new dial and new wiring. Nothing helps and they admit they are frustrated. Any suggestions?

With a new dash gauge installed, the problem most probably is at the other end of the circuit. Either the float arm in the fuel tank is bent or the tank sender unit is defective. The sending unit must be removed, checked and replaced (Fig. 16-4). There is one other possibility and that is if a malfunctioning voltage regulator is not delivering constant voltage to the unit, in which case the regulator must be replaced.

Can you tell me the capacity of the fuel tank on the 1972 Pinto Runabout with 122-cubic-inch engine and air conditioning? My owner's manual says the Pinto has an 11-gallon tank (12 on station wagons). Recently, I asked for a fillup at a gas station and the attendant charged me $10 for 16.4 gallons of gas. The station owner tried to tell me I had a 24-gallon tank. I told him his pump was wrong. I complained to (the state bureau of) weights and measures and they later told me the pump was off and they shut it down.

Your service manual is correct. Pinto fuel tanks have an 11-gallon capacity, except for the station wagons, which are 12. The fact that state inspectors determined that the station's pump was incorrect is of little solace to you now that you've spent the money.

Anyone who runs into a situation like this — and it happens, usually in a much more subtle way, more often than most of us realize—should do one of two things.

The best way to handle it is to flatly refuse to pay the bill. Even if the operator should summon the police, it won't take the officer very long to figure out who is trying to do what to whom.

If you don't want the hassle involved but still want to arm yourself with evidence for later use, insist on a written (and signed) receipt before handing over the money. Make sure the receipt shows the exact gallons dispensed as well as the total money paid.

Last June, I ordered a new Chevrolet half-ton Silverado pickup truck. At that time, I took the salesman outside and showed him the various things I wanted on the truck from ones that were on the lot. I took delivery two months later and it had the wrong mirrors, bumpers, and seat. They put the correct bumpers on but now the mirrors are rusting. The dealer offered to paint the mirrors or replace them with chrome ones (which I ordered in the first place) for $30. I can't get any response on the seat. Can you offer any advice?

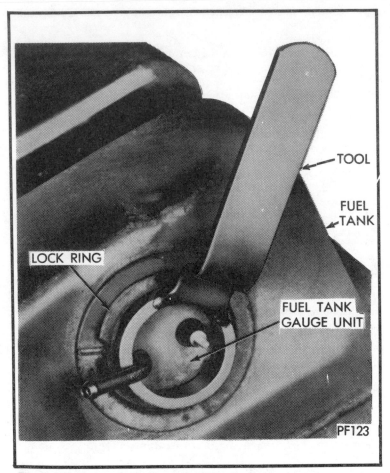

Fig. 16-4. In most applications, a special ring-like tool is necessary to extricate the sender unit from the fuel tank. (Courtesy Chrysler Corp.)

At this point, I don't see much of anything that you can do. What you should have done in the first place was refuse to take delivery (i.e. hang on to your money) until the truck was equipped the way you ordered it. Once a seller has your money in his hands, he is a lot less likely to act on minor complaints such as yours. Actually, I think you were fortunate in getting him to change the bumpers, and the deal he is offering you on the mirrors seems reasonable enough. Chalk it up to experience.

I'd appreciate some specific pointers about how a person can protect his car from being stolen. Could you also indicate if there really are useful devices or gadgets that can stop most would-be crooks? Also, where can the best devices be bought and installed? Since I recently had a new car stolen and I was lucky enough to get most of it back within a few days (it was partially stripped), I'm

very concerned about protecting my car as much as possible from being stolen again.

Unfortunately, there is no completely foolproof way to protect a car from being stolen, especially if the person who is after it is a professional car thief. If a pro wants your car, he'll get it. And there is quite a bit of that going on these days, especially in cars that fall into the unusual or luxury class. Most of the warning devices you mention are worthless unless you live in a quiet neighborhood where there are genuinely concerned neighbors. Most of the whistle, siren, horn-blowing anti-theft units are worthless because the average person is going to ignore it. And, a good car thief can have this device disconnected about as fast as he can get your car started—which is about equal to the time it takes you to unlock your car and get it going with the key.

There are interrupt systems that will slow a thief and stop an amateur. These include in-line fuel shut-off valves (which a pro will recognize immediately because the fuel gauge will register anyway) and a coil shut-off switch. The best solution is to keep your car in a safe place, preferably a locked garage, so as to keep it from being a target in the first place.

As a traveling field representative, I was apprehensive of adequate gasoline supplies or rationing. So when General Motors advertised the virtues of the Astre (or Vega) with a 140-cubic-inch engine as giving up to 37 miles per gallon (EPA rated), I hastened to buy an Astre.

I now get only 20 mpg doing most of my driving at 50 mph on highways (and) my car initially didn't run right. I got some of the problems corrected. What hasn't been corrected is the performance of the new four-cylinder engine.

I wrote several letters of complaint to the chairman of GM and received one reply from a "consumer" representative telling me to take the car to the original dealer or select another.

Although the advertisement to which you refer clearly stipulates—as do all promotions referring to EPA mileage figures—that the mileage you get can vary depending on the type and style of driving you do, 20 mpg does sound low.

Chapter 17

Oldies but Goodies:

Antique and Classic Cars

We have a dear elderly friend who is sickly and in need of cash. She has a 1950 Dodge four-door sedan with 52,340 original miles. It always has been kept in a garage. The car is in excellent condition and is run regularly to keep things operating.

We think selling this car could be a big help to her. Could you give us a fair appraisal of its possible value?

I do not believe the car is worth as much as you are hoping. According to Hemming's Motor News, which is the bible of antique and classic auto collectors, the car is probably worth less than $500. I base this estimate on the fact that in the June issue there was an advertisement to sell for $400 a 1950 Dodge Meadowbrook four-door sedan. One difference, however, was that the car registered only 35,000 miles. All other things being equal, that would make it worth more.

Years ago, my father bought a McFarland car second hand. It was a four-door sedan. I believe it was a custom-made car and I'd like to know more about them. They never seem to be in any of the big car books or at antique car shows. The purchase was made between 1928 and 1930.

I believe you are referring to a car called the McFarlan, which was built in Connersville, Ind., by the McFarlan Carriage Company, starting in 1902. Although the company changed its name to McFarlan Motor Corp. and later to McFarlan Motor Car Co., it continued to build cars through 1928. As for being custom-built, that's probably true since many companies in those days provided chassis and running gear from independent coach builders.

I am in the process of restoring a 1960 Austin-Healey and would like to know the address of any Austin-Healy clubs. I also would appreciate the name of any shops that might carry new or reconditioned parts for this car.

Fig. 17-1. When finished, a good restoration should look exactly like this new 1960 Austin-Healey. (Courtesy British-Leyland)

The only Austin Healey Club in the country, according to British-Leyland Motors which is the successor to the company that built your car, can be contacted through Box 6267, San Jose, Calif. 95150. For additional information, you might contact Fred Horner, in care of British-Leyland, 600 Willow Tree Rd., Leonia, N.J., 07605. See Fig. 17-1.

My brother and I collect the small, two-seater sports cars known as the AMX that were produced by American Motors. These cars were only built for three years and were supposed to be a very limited production vehicle. But there seem to be thousands of them in the greater Cleveland area alone. I estimate that between 1968 and 1970, production must have run close to 35,000 units, but I've been unable to find the actual figures. Could you determine what the actual production run of the AMX was in each year?

According to the folks at American Motors, you guesstimate is very high. When compared with your figure of 35,000, the AMX was truly a limited production. When the little car debuted in 1968, 6,725 were built. It enjoyed its biggest success in 1969 with 8,293 units. In 1970, it tailed off to 4,116 for a total 3-year run of 19,134 cars. That might sound like a lot of cars, but when compared with the normal Detroit production figures, it's hardly a drop in the bucket. The AMC people came to the same conclusion that Ford had 13 years earlier—that there was more of a market for a four-seat personal car than a two-seater. Thus the Javelin replaced the AMX in the lineup. Ironically, the Javelin became history in 1974 because it didn't meet federal rollover standards.

Can you tell me who I could contact to get body parts for an antique (1940) La Salle? Any help would be appreciated.

From the tone of your letter, I gather that you've exhausted every lead. As you know, parts of any type for prewar cars are getting harder and harder to find. One solution I can suggest is to contact the Complete Cadillac Parts Co., 512 Birch Hollow Drive, Shirley, N.Y., 11967. They claim to have the most complete stock of parts for Cadillacs and La Salles dating from 1937 through 1948. If you don't have any success there, you might want to contact Hemmings Motor News, Box 380, Bennington, VT., 05201, which has the most complete selection of classified ads for antique and classic cars that I have ever seen.

I am in dire need of an emergency brake cable for my 1948 pickup truck. All of the local parts dealers laugh when I ask them for one. Where can I turn?

Not knowing the brand of vehicle you own I can't give you any specifics. However, as a first step I would advise writing to the customer-service division of the company that made the truck. Other possibilities are the Antique Automobile Club of America, whose members have parts for cars most of us never even heard of, or the flea markets that always accompany the various antique and classical car shows. Another is the J. C. Whitney of Chicago or a similar mail-order parts supplier. I am sure you'll be able to get the exact part or a similar one that will be adaptable.

I have a four-door Corvair purchased the year they first came out—1960. Can you tell me if it's worth anything to an automobile collector?

There's no doubt in my mind that it is worth "something" to a collector. It's even worth something as a used car in today's economy-conscious market. How much it's worth is an entirely different story. If it is in good condition with relatively low mileage, the car could be worth a fair amount—several hundred dollars. But even if it's in poor shape, I am sure a Corvair buff would be willing to give you at least someting for it even if he just wanted it as a parts car—spares for one or more others. You might be able to get a better idea by contacting Mark Ellis in care of the Corvair Society of America, 145 Ivywood Lane, Radnor, Pa.

Quite awhile ago, you advised the owner of a 1965 Mustang to keep it as it would become a classic with a value of $3,000 or more by 1978. I also took your advice to heart and have kept mine in mint condition—mileage now 79,200. In view of current inflation, what would you say my car is now worth? How about in a year or two?

A combination of factors, led by inflations, has accelerated the rate of appreciation of many classic cars. A recent edition of Hemmings Motor News lists several 1965 Mustangs from $950 to over $2,000, depending on mileage and condition. And 1966s are worth almost as much, while even the 1967s are reaping the benefit.

If you car is in mint condition as you say, it's probably worth upwards of $1,500—but not on the normal market. If you want to sell, you had better advertise directly to the collector market. As for the future, there's no way the car will depreciate in value. That goes for any car that has started to appreciate. And the state of the economy will have very little effect. It seems, in times of stress, collectors are willing to spend even more money.

I have a 1963 Thunderbird in mint condition and am wondering what its approximate value might be. I have been told it's a collector's item because of the excellent shape it is in. It's been babied all of its life and is mechanically like new. There isn't a scratch on the car and everything works, right down to the power seat. Could you please give me a general idea of its value so I don't undersell myself?

Generally speaking, Thunderbirds of that era are worth between $1,000 and $3,000, depending not only on overall condition, but on the car's acutal mileage. For example, I recently saw a very nice 1963 hardtop (Fig. 17-2) with 75,000 miles on it go for $1,050. The car showed some signs of use but by no means had been abused. I own a 1961 Bird that is in need of a fair amount of body work on the sides—the doors and quarter panels are banged up pretty well—but has less than 16,000 original miles. I have turned down an offer of $1,200 (believing the man would have gone higher) simply because I have no desire to get rid of the car at any price.

All Thunderbirds built between 1955 and 1966 are commanding higher than normal prices. The two-seaters built between 1955 and 1957 are bringing the most money—some as high as $10,000. The 1961 through 1963 models—especially the roadsters with a hard tonneau cover—are next most valuable.

I have a 1965 Marlin that now has 60,000 miles on it and still runs as good as the day I bought it. This car has had very few repairs other than normal maintenance. I would like to know how many were built in 1965 and each year after the first edition.

You are the proud owner of a rare, if not classic, automobile. The Marlin, introduced as a 1965 model in the fall of 1964, was American Motors' first venture into the "sporty" car market. Although based mainly on the Rambler sedans of that era, the Marlin had a sporty, if somewhat bulky, look with its fastback styling.

In the first year of production, AMC cranked out 10,327 copies. In 1966 production fell to 4,547, and in 1967 it dropped even further to 2,545, for a three-year total of 17,419.

The car was replaced in the American Motors lineup by the two-seater AMX in 1968. That car later was replaced by the Javelin, which, when it became history two years ago, left AMC without a sporty-type car.

I am trying to decide whether or not to buy my neighbor's 1967 Lincoln four-door convertible. It has been driven about 38,000 miles and has always been garaged since he bought it new. It has all the powers, AM-FM radio with tape deck, radial tires and is in excellent running condition.

He is asking $3,000, and I have been told this is a special interest car that could be held for future sale. I'd like to know about what it's worth and whether its value might increase.

If the car is as good as you say it is, $3,000, is more than a fair price for a car that undoubtedly will appreciate with time. How valuable it becomes is a matter of conjecture.

I have seen several of these car advertised of late, with prices up to $4,000. However, keep in mind that the value of a specific car is what the traffic will bear.

There are many people with a penchant for prewar cars who wouldn't, if you'll excuse the expression, give you a plugged nickel for the later model classic car.

We recently purchased a 1976 Cadillac DeVille. At the time of purchase, one of the salesmen told us this car will be worth more in three years time than the price we paid for it new. Could this be true?

If I knew for sure that that would be the case, I'd get a second mortage and start grabbing up all the 1976s I could find. There are two schools of thought regarding the appreciation of cars that have gone out of production.

First, if public acceptance of the new models runs as high as General Motors predicts—and early sales reports so indicate—then the older ones will just sort of assume their proper place in the used car market.

I think you will find that 1976 Cadillacs, especially the Coupe DeVilles, will become collectors' items, but I don't think it will happen overnight the way it did for 1976 Cadillac Eldorado convertibles.

Your car will depreciate at something less than the normal rate for a few years and then begin to become more valuable, assuming that it is kept in top-flight condition and not driven to excess.

As I see it, the only way it will be worth more in three years than you paid for it is if inflation becomes rampant—and the economists tell us that isn't likely.

We own a 1964 Buick Riviera that is in excellent running condition and has about 75,000 miles on it. This car is absolutely the best driving and most comfortable car we have ever owned.

150

Fig. 17-2. Thunderbirds like this 1963 hardtop (as shown in original 1963 publicity release photo) are appreciating faster than most of the so-called late-model classics. (Courtesy Ford Motor Company)

We are hesitant about taking it on any long trips in case it develops major trouble and we are far from home and familiar repair service. Primarily we just take it on short runs to give it exercise.

We'd like to know how much care to give it. We presume it will increase in value but are hesitant to make a major investment should it become necessary. Would we be better off using it or putting it on blocks?

Since you obviously enjoy driving the car a great deal, I certainly wouldn't put it on blocks just in the hope of getting a few more dollars for it at some undetermined time.

I also wouldn't concern myself with how much I might have to spend on repairs that may or may not be necessary: If the car has been properly cared for over the years, 75,000 miles is no reason for you to be afraid to use it. I have owned cars with more mileage than that that I wouldn't have been afraid to drive across the country.

Assuming you have a mechanic that you deal with regularly and trust, have him give the car a thorough going-over to make sure it is sound. If so, drive and enjoy.

As to the car's potential value, I don't think it's as high as you might hope. Right now, Rivieras of that vintage are going from $2,500 for a fully restored car down to $1,000 or less.

Sure would like to know what our old Studebaker truck that grandpa left is worth. No one seems to know. It is a 1959 pickup with a 6-foot bed. It is a V-8 with standard transmission, 40,000 miles and excellent condition. It has been repainted once professionally.

We've checked local books, magazines and newspapers but trucks of this vintage aren't listed—only cars. Do you have any ideas?

I think you're in that never-never land of whatever the market will bear. If you find someone who really wants it, it could be worth several hundred dollars. Strictly as a pickup truck, it is nothing more than a 20-year-old vehicle worth a few hundred at most.

Since my husband died two years ago, our 1956 Ford Victoria has been sitting in the garage. The tires have deflated and there's some liquid on the floor. I am anxious to sell it and would like to get $500. Any ideas?

Without seeing the car or knowing anything about its condition, it is hard to put a price on it. However, there is demand among collectors for that type of car. If it's restorable, it's worth at least $500 and maybe a lot more.

My daughter owns a 1971 Volvo P-1800 with about 50,000 miles on it. She now wishes to buy an Oldsmobile Starfire but understands that her Volvo is worth a lot now and, in the future, may be worth a lot more.

Should she keep the Volvo (the money is no big thing now) and hope the value goes up or should she sell it now? If she keeps it, I have room in my garage.

If she should keep it, is there anything in particular she would have to do to keep it in good condition for resale later?

Right now, this out-of-production model is bringing about $3,000 on the used car market and about $1,800 on a trade-in. With that kind of a differential, I wouldn't trade it in unless I also got a big discount on the list price of the new car.

The P-1800, which was last produced as a sports coupe in 1973, is one of those cars that should appreciate on the collector's market. There are two reasons for this. First and most importantly, there weren't very many of them imported, giving them exclusivity. Secondly, the design was both unique and attractive—a strong selling point.

If money is no object, I would keep the car as an investment. Among the things I would do is to have the engine compartment and the entire undercarriage steam-cleaned to remove all dirt and grime. The outside should be cleaned and waxed and the inside should get a thorough scrubbing.

Then, it would be advisable to have it completely serviced—lubrication, oil change, and tune-up—before putting it in the garage on blocks and under a cover. This might cost upwards of $150, but you'll more than get it back when you sell it.

I own one of the first 1971 production model Eldorado convertibles (it has many vents in the trunk lid, later 1971s had fewer vents.) The engine is very good but the body needs work. I understand that once the 1976 Eldorado convertibles become "older used cars" that the 1971s, being the first of the last convertible models, will then become even more valuable. Do you think that this is true? Should I spend serious money to fix my 1971?

I don't think that the great amount of 1976 Eldorado convertibles ever will fall into the "older used car" category because the majority of the production run was grabbed up by collectors and investors.

As of right now, 1976 Eldorados with less than 1,000 miles on them are bringing up to $20,000. A nice profit for a car that listed for less than $12,000 when new.

As for your car, it certainly will appreciate with time. Current value is in the $3,000 to $4,000 range. As for spending serious money, I don't think I'd go much over $1,000.

I have a 1969 Corvette with a 427 engine. The car is used only occasionally, and I keep it in great shape. I would like to know if it's best for the car to start it once a week and drive it, start it and just let the engine warm up, or just start it when I am going to use it, which might be only once every six to eight weeks.

There are various schools of thought on this subject, ranging from use a car as regularly as possible to put it up on blocks after draining all liquids.

I'll tell you what I do with my low-mileage vintage Thunderbird. Whenever the weather permits, I take the car out for an hour or so of highway driving about twice a month. This seems to keep everything working the way it should and also has kept the battery with enough power to start it under the worst temperature conditions. Also, I change the oil and filter twice a year (even though I put on less than 1,000 mile a year) and, at the same time, I lubricate the chassis. And I wash it regularly, including a high-pressure hosedown of fenderwells.

The only thing I wouldn't do is start the engine and just let it warm up and idle. This helps to build up condensation and acids which break down the engine oil and cause undue wear and tear. You would be better off not running it at all. No matter what, oil should be changed at least twice a year.

Index